Managing to Survive

Managing to Survive

Working Lives in Small Firms

Monder Ram

Copyright © Basil Blackwell, 1994

First published 1994

Blackwell Publishers
108 Cowley Road
Oxford
OX4 1JF
UK

238 Main Street
Cambridge, Massachusetts 02142
USA

British Library Cataloging in Publication Data

A CIP catalogue record for this book is available from the British Library.

Library of Congress Cataloguing-in-Publication Data

A CIP catalog record for this book is available from the Library of Congress.

ISBN 0-631-191097

Prepared on PageMaker in 10 on 11pt Palatino by Simone Dudley, Industrial Relations Research Unit, University of Warwick, CV4 7AL, Coventry.

Printed in Great Britain by T.J. Press Ltd, Padstow, Cornwall.

To my Mother and Father, with thanks.

Contents

Series Editors' Foreword

The University of Warwick is the major centre in the United Kingdom for the study of industrial relations. Teaching of the subject began in 1966 in the School of Industrial and Business Studies, which now has one of the country's largest graduate programmes. Warwick became a national centre for research in industrial relations in 1970 when the Social Science Research Council (now the Economic and Social Research Council) established its Industrial Relations Research Unit at the University. In 1984 the Unit was reconstituted as a Designated Research Centre within the School of Industrial and Business Studies. It continues to be known as the Industrial Relations Research Unit, however, and it now embraces the research activities of all members of the School's industrial relations community.

The series of Warwick Studies in Industrial Relations was launched in 1972 by Hugh Clegg and George Bain as the main vehicle for the publication of the results of the Unit's research projects, as well as the research conducted by staff teaching industrial relations in the University and the work of graduate students. The first six titles were published by Heinemann Educational Books of London, and subsequent volumes have been published by Blackwell Publishers of Oxford.

The present work is based on Monder Ram's doctoral thesis. The thesis impressed everyone who read it with its fascinating analysis of a little-known world and with the clarity of its message. This book carries forward these strengths while also drawing out the wider implications of the study. It builds on the Unit's long-established tradition of workplace studies by applying tested research methods to new areas.

As Monder Ram indicates, the book addresses debates concerning the role of small firms in economic regeneration and the nature of ethnic minority businesses. But its core is the analysis of what actually goes on inside small firms. Drawing on his unrivalled knowledge of the industry, the author shows the errors of conventional assumptions, which characterise workplace relations as being either on harmony or on autocracy. In their place, he identifies a pattern of 'negotiated paternalism' and explores its complex dynamics. In the conclusion, he relates this pattern to existing workplace studies, demonstrating the conditions under which it is likely to exist. In the course of this analysis, he explores the nature of managerial activity. Again developing other Unit work, he shows how management is a continuous and uncertain process and that apparently rational solutions may be irrational when viewed in the context of a firm's social dynamics. The book is a rich ethnography but also an explanation of why relationships operated as they did.

The book thus addresses many important debates. It will be of particular relevance to students of workplace industrial relations and industrial sociology and of management as well as specialists in the field of small firms. The richness of its account of working lives will interest anyone concerned to know how work is experienced.

Paul Edwards
Richard Hyman
Keith Sisson

Acknowledgements

This book would have been extremely difficult to complete without the assistance of others along the way. I would like to thank Paul Edwards and Annie Phizacklea for their constructive comments on previous drafts of this work. The time and support afforded by my sponsor organisation, the University of Central England in Birmingham was also much appreciated. I am further grateful to the workers and managers who co-operated in the research for this book; they put up with my presence with good humour while they themselves were often stuck in a tedious and trying world. The final and greatest debt is to my parents, who have toiled hard and made so much possible. Their unstinting and unconditional support was, and remains, precious.

1

Introduction

What is it like being an Asian businessman running a small firm in the clothing industry? How do you deal with customers and suppliers? How do you persuade workers to work long hours for low pay and yet produce goods on time and at the right price? Above all, how do you keep the firm going from one day to the next in the face of intense product market competition and ever-present uncertainties on the shopfloor?

This book examines a hitherto unexplored world. Focusing on the Asian and small-firm-dominated West Midlands clothing industry, the study explores the reality of life on the shopfloor for many managers and workers engaged in a previously neglected yet crucial part of the small firm sector. Its insights stem from the author's unique position: as an insider with years of experience working in the industry who has stepped outside it to analyse its dynamics and relate it to its context. The case itself is based on a year-long study of three firms in the West Midlands, but the author also draws on his experience as a manager and consultant in the sector to provide an in-depth account of how small firms actually work.

The study combines a detailed portrait of a distinctive sector with analysis which uses the case study to address wider debates. One such debate turns on the place of small firms in the economy. For some, these firms are crucial to job creation and entrepreneurial values. A related view focuses on flexible specialisation, arguing that it is possible to carve out a profitable niche based on high quality products and sophisticated design. The study seriously questions this optimistic scenario. A rich and detailed picture of how small firms operate on a day-to-day basis is developed. The particular processes, calculations and negotiations involved in managing the workplace are examined; and this allows analysis of how changes in a conspicuously turbulent environment are managed on the shopfloor. What becomes clear is that the scope to move to a flexible specialisation model is crucially affected by a number of considerations, including a volatile market and a lack of investment funds. Such forces heavily influence management's room for manoeuvre.

A more realistic approach to examining small firms in such contexts is to focus, as many have done, on the ethnic background of employers. This literature stresses that Asians are in the clothing sector not because of any cultural flair for enterprise but because of the lack of alternative opportunities. The study confirms this picture, but also goes much further by exploring how the conflicting pressures of ethnicity are managed. For example, a major concern of managers was a limited supply of labour, even though they were in a depressed area with considerable unemployment. The reason for the apparent contradiction was a set of assumptions about what type of worker was suitable. Employers looked for female workers of Asian origin who had experience of the industry. To have looked further afield would have brought in workers whom it might have been difficult to manage. This point leads to the heart of the study, the way in which the shopfloor was managed.

One view is that the workplace is harmonious. An alternative paints a picture of autocracy. For both, this case study offers a critical test case. The firms were small, most of the workers were women, and there were many family ties between managers and workers. For the first view, these characteristics should promote close working relationships. For the second, they are likely to lead to the domination of workers by managers.

The adequacy of both views is questioned in the light of the study. Instead, a more realistic analysis around the concept of 'negotiated paternalism' is developed. This analysis suggests that the process of establishing order at the workplace involves many forms of negotiation, not the simple imposition of managerial demands. Although small firms operating in this sector are subject to intense competition and engage in allegedly widespread practices like the evasion of statutory duties and the utilisation of homeworkers, autocracy on the shopfloor is not necessarily the inevitable consequence. Rather, it is important to focus on the processes involved in negotiating order at the workplace. This focus suggests a more complex picture in which management needs to harness workers' skills and somehow balance a range of conflicting pressures. The result is neither autocracy nor harmony, but a situation in which negotiated obligations are constructed and re-constructed.

Finally, the study explores the place of ethnic characteristics within the workplace. The West Midlands clothing sector is dominated by Asians, but what is the significance of this background? Some writers see ethnicity as having no special role. Others argue that it is a further managerial resource, with the status order of Asian caste systems being used to regulate workers of low caste. A closer exploration of ethnicity in the study highlights that existing views do not adequately explain its influence at the level of the workplace. Ethnicity is shown to be a complex resource whose effects also had to be negotiated. Moreover, it could not stand apart from gender and familial connections.

It is clear then that the West Midlands clothing industry comprises particular features of considerable importance to the subject of workplace relations in small firms. The sector is at the interstices of a number of related issues, namely, concrete restructuring trajectories of small firms, management organisation and ethnicity.

The examination of how these issues interact and are played out on the shopfloor has important implications for the research design. If the vicissitudes and the nuances of the shopfloor are to be picked up, understood and properly interpreted, there needs to be a certain intimacy with the workplace and an awareness of the importance of its cultural context and specificities. In short, empathy and close proximity to the research site are methodological imperatives. It is only in this way that one can disentangle the logic behind the seemingly bizarre nature of workplace behaviour and so pierce the veneer of 'rationality' that so effectively masks the operations of such firms.

The actual way in which the research was conducted is set out in detail in chapter two, but it is appropriate here to signal the importance of my own background to the study. I am an Asian man and part of a large extended family that has been thoroughly immersed in the clothing industry in different capacities for nearly twenty years. I have worked for the family business (which forms one of the case study firms in the research) for a number of years and for local agencies on projects designed to assist the garment industry. Consequently, my ethnic, familial and working background is essentially the same as those who form the focus of the current study. I am therefore fortunate that I can view the salient issues from a privileged vantage point.

Crucial though these life experiences are to eliciting 'quality' data, the research is more than an exercise in simply 'telling it how it is'. My background has also embraced academia and my current occupation is that of a lecturer/ researcher. The combination of being simultaneously on the 'inside' and the 'outside' provides a unique opportunity to dig deep into the rationalities of the shopfloor and unearth its logics. Hopefully then, I can offer a genuine insider's perspective that is suitably apprised of the importance of wider debates and issues.

The remainder of the chapter is organised around the three main themes of the study. The first section examines how the concept of the negotiation of order has been treated within existing accounts of the clothing sector. This is followed by a consideration of the nature of management and the adequacy of the managerial autocracy view of the governance of small firms. The final section flags up the importance of ethnicity to workplace relations in the West Midlands clothing industry and assesses how it has been presented within studies of ethnic enterprise and the labour process debate.

The Negotiation of Order

The term 'negotiation of order' is used here to indicate the central processes at work on the shopfloor. It signifies a concern with the informal, as well formal, aspects of workplace relations and stresses the importance of accommodation and struggle. Braverman's (1984) emphasis on deskilling and the degradation of work left out of the equation the informal nature of workplace relations and the ways in which workers could modify, if not resist, capitalists' control. However, in seeking to address this omission, subsequent studies have tended to counterpose managerial control with strategies of resistance (for example, Gordon et al, 1982). In doing so, such approaches again tend to neglect the informal and dynamic processes that shape shopfloor relations (for detailed criticism, see Nolan and Edwards, 1984).

A concern with the processes, pressures and complexities on the shopfloor does not, however, imply a voluntarist approach to workplace relations - it does not mean that structural conditions do not influence behaviour. Edwards (1986) and Hyman (1987) have offered a way of conceptualising relations at work that acknowledges the importance of structural conditions without being deterministic, and allows for action but within certain constraints. This view suggests that inherent within the employment relationship is a basic antagonism between capital and labour. Together with this basic antagonism, however, are elements of co-operation since employers need to secure workers' willingness to work while workers rely on firms for their livelihoods. This fundamental antagonism does not actually determine events since they have to be interpreted in action. A negotiation of order occurs but within a definite material context.

Using this approach to analyse the fundamentals of workplace relations, it is clear that, in the context of the West Midlands clothing industry, a number of salient features need to be assessed in order to examine how they interact and shape events on the shopfloor. For example, issues like the market, firm size, management organisation, family, gender and ethnicity - all factors that impact upon the negotiation of order - need to be explored in order to flesh out the dynamics of workplace relations. Take, for instance, the issue of 'rate-fixing'; in many accounts of the clothing industry (Westwood, 1984, for example) it is regarded as almost exclusively the preserve of management and a prime indicator of autocracy. But what are the factors that govern the setting of the rate and are the outcomes as authoritarian as commonly portrayed ? In the context of the West Midlands clothing industry, the calculation of the rate needs to be viewed as the product of conflicting pressures like the volatility of the market, custom and practice, machinists' priorities and preferences, the availability of external labour, the state of the labour market and ethnicity. The eventual outcome will reflect the relative importance of these factors and formal and informal negotiations on the shopfloor.

There has, however, been very little in the way of substantive analysis of processual aspects of the construction of order at the workplace in the West Midlands clothing sector or similar kinds of firms. Many profiles of the industry in the region (of which Leigh and North, 1983 is the most comprehensive) merely sketch out particular characteristics of the local sector - its recent growth, domination by the Asian community, the preponderance of very small firms (under thirty employees) and the widespread evasion of statutory duties. Beyond these generalities, however, there seems to be little evidence of what actually goes on in the workplace. These profiles, taken together with relatively rare studies like Hoel's (1984) rather anecdotal account of women workers in Coventry 'sweatshops', appear to confirm the general image of the sector, namely, one of the barely mitigated coercive nature of workplace relations.

The theme of informality and negotiation on the shopfloor has certainly featured in some studies of the garment industry, but it appears that management were most emphatically in the ascendency. In Armstrong et al's study (1981) of a footwear manufacturer, for example, management certainly had to engage in processes that would legitimate their actions;

they were concerned with notions of 'fairness' and 'legitimacy'. But workers rarely questioned the employer's right to manage and the primacy of profitability. Supervision was close and the pace of work intense. Although informal rules and activities did develop, management could tackle them when they posed a threat, and furthermore, such activities were not always contrary to management's interests. Similarly, in Edwards and Scullion's study (1982) of Hosiery and Underwear Factories, there was strict enforcement of discipline on the shopfloor with workers being discouraged from moving from their work stations and conversing with their colleagues. In large part this was deemed necessary to meet the quality and delivery targets that were pre-requisites for surviving in a competitive market.

Cunnison's study (1966) of the Dee waterproof garment company goes much further in highlighting the flexibly negotiated nature of the employment relationship. The mutual dependency between workers and managers was evident as managers had to go to some lengths to keep workers satisfied, in particular by ensuring a steady supply of work. Given the rapid and unforeseeable fluctuations in the market, management had the difficult task of keeping a steady flow of work while meeting urgent orders.

Taken together, these studies give a flavour of how order is established on the shopfloor, but, Cunnison notwithstanding, they tend to reinforce the role of management as the overwhelmingly dominant party. Moreover, in terms of relevance for the current study, they take place in much larger settings than clothing firms in the West Midlands and they do not address the question of ethnicity. However, the issue of work relations in small firms, if not ethnicity, has been the focus of increased attention in recent years.

Workplace Relations in Small Firms

There is a comparatively large body of literature (see Scase and Goffee, 1987, for example) that has explored the motives, difficulties and prospects of small business owners. However, until relatively recently, much less was known about employment relations in small firms. Yet, despite the lack of evidence, there seemed to be a popular view that small firms were usually characterised by 'harmonious' employment relations since their was little indication of overt industrial conflict. This image was based largely on Ingham's (1970) 'industrial harmony' thesis, which suggested that employees in small firms exhibited a high degree of attachment to their workplace and worked in such establishments primarily for nonmaterial reasons. Ingham's evidence was used by the Bolton Report of 1971 to affirm the view that industrial relations in small firms were non-problematic. Such images have fitted conveniently into the attempts by Conservative governments during the 1980s to promote small businesses as economic catalysts and thoroughly decent places to work in. The Government latched on to these visions of industrial harmony and placed small businesses at the vanguard of entrepreneurial activity.

The relatively few empirical investigations into small firms have inflicted serious damage on the rather fragile industrial harmony thesis. Studies by Stanworth and Curran (1981) and Goss (1988), for example, have shown that workplace relations in small firms are far from harmonious. Most recently, Rainnie (1989) has focused on the printing and clothing industries to demonstrate his contention that industrial relations in small firms are somewhat less than 'beautiful'. Since the clothing industry is central to Rainnie's basic thesis, it would be apt to consider his study in more detail.

Rainnie attempts a considered analysis of the position of small firms in the economy, the relationship between large and small firms, and the centrality of competition and its impact on industrial relations. Far from being the answer to Britain's employment problems and the most favoured places of employment, small firms are shown to be amongst the most vulnerable in the economy, often dangerous places to work in and arenas of authoritarian workplace relations.

Rainnie's analysis is undoubtedly a useful corrective to the widespread eulogising of the alleged virtues of small businesses. However, there is a tendency in the reaction against the 'small is beautiful' shibboleth to view small firms as little more than sites of managerial autocracy. This tendency is evident in Rainnie's account of the small-firm-dominated clothing sector, an analysis that attaches primacy to competition.

According to Rainnie, there are two essential elements to an adequate explanation of the labour process :

1.   " The complex and uneven nature of the development of capital and the effect this has on the development of the labour process
2.   The varied response of labour to these developments " (p53).

In analysing the complex and uneven nature of capital, Rainnie contends that competition and the small firm-large firm relationship are crucial to understanding the demands placed on individual capitalists, and hence, the way in which work is organised. The fortunes of clothing manufacturers are closely linked to those of the major retailers, who account for 70%

of their production. These retailers are in a position to squeeze the margins of manufacturers in periods of recession and uncertainty. The garment industry is then characterised by an uneven distribution of power between retailers and domestic manufacturers. The effect of this imbalance of power is such that certain retailers, notably Marks and Spencer, effectively control manufacturers. In times of heightened competition, it is these manufacturers that suffer from the dependent nature of such a relationship. For Rainnie then, the large firm-small firm setting largely explains the British clothing industry's continued reliance on cheap female labour and low-level technology.

The influence of retailers should not be underestimated. Their increasingly fluid buying patterns have a significant impact on the fortunes of individual garment manufacturers (Totterdil and Zeitlin, 1989). Rainnie, however, seems to suggest that these developments have a deterministic effect on the labour process. Competition, especially in the context of the clothing industry, is certainly an important causal influence on the labour process, but for Rainnie, it appears to be an invariant one. He argues that the particular form that the extraction of surplus value will take within small firms can only be explained if competition is regarded as a crucial determining factor in the drive to accumulate, " The competition to obtain regular outlets for long runs is great and costs have to be controlled. Clothing is a labour intensive industry.... The result is tight managerial control over a system that dictates the pace of work " (p217). Furthermore, such competition leads to "a more brutal form of management".

The actual case study evidence upon which such general claims concerning the shape of workplace relations are based seems rather patchy. There are many assertions about the seemingly coercive nature of managerial control but they appear to be in the form of general statements rather than interpretation of concrete events. The result is a rather one-dimensional, almost linear view of workplace control, as the following quotation illustrates... " Discipline is necessary to get potential labour turned into actual labour. The driving force behind this being profit, a force that instils a tight fistedness in all owner managers, particularly in times of heightened competition " (p116).

An account that acknowledges the importance of competition is to be welcomed since "it places the management of employee relations within its corporate context, explicitly acknowledging that control over the labour process is not the sole or prime concern of employers, but is generally subsidiary to the achievement of broader company goals" (Marchington, 1990:111). The way in which work is organised at the point of production does not represent the whole circuit of capital and does not provide an adequate account of the production, realisation and accumulation of surplus value. Management is often just as concerned with the development of favourable conditions for the realisation of surplus value in the product market as with securing optimum conditions for the creation of surplus value through the labour process (Knights and Wilmott, 1986).

There is, however, a difference between acknowledging the importance of competition and suggesting, as Rainnie does, that it has a determinant role. Competition, like other external influences, cannot be regarded as independent or distinct from what happens in the labour process. It does not have a determinate effect, rather, it needs to be interpreted in action, and this will depend on the social relations of production. Competition may shape work relations, but it is doubtful if it actually determines them. Employers and workers are not passive in the midst of such forces. They have their own struggles, and the particular form that these struggles will take cannot be predicted in advance. Structural conditions such as the nature of the product market serve only to provide broad constraints or opportunities. Their precise effect will be contingent upon the manner in which the labour process is organised (Edwards, 1986).

An example demonstrating the varying impact of competition is provided by Kochan, McKersie and Cappelli (1984) in their analysis of the way in which American tyre companies responded to the introduction of radials on to the tyre market. Each of the major tyre companies adopted a different competitive strategy and each had different implications for the management of labour. Goodyear decided to compete across all markets and opened up non-union plants to reduce costs; Firestone opted to consolidate by closing certain lines, although they remained in the market and generated competition between different plants; Goodrich moved out of the tyre market completely, but remained on good terms with its employees through its policy of diversification; Uniroyal embarked upon a drastic cost cutting exercise, closing three of its five plants and encountering much union opposition in the process. These examples illustrate that the market does have an important effect on employee relations, but its eventual impact will be conditioned by the interaction with other processes, which in these cases included the decisions of senior managers.

It is, moreover, unlikely that a particular factor can be singled out as the key cause of difference in the pattern of work relations. There is an interplay which militates against the isolation of discrete factors. "Effects work together such that there are clusters of characteristics whose separate components cannot be pulled apart" (Edwards, 1986: 75). In the context of the clothing industry, can competition be seen as decisive when the state of the labour market, gender, racism and technical gradualism have been so important in the shaping of workplace relations? Parmar makes a similar point in her study of Asian women's exploitation and 'resistance' in Britain. She claims that capitalism, patriarchy and racism structure Asian women's exploitation and this renders it impossible and undesirable to separate out the primary cause of that exploitation (1982:239). In responding to and accommodating this exploitation, Asian women draw upon resources from their specific cultural tradition, their strength as a collectivity and their importance to the firm as workers.

There can be little doubt that management in Rainnie's study were coercive, but even in these situations where discipline and supervision is undoubtedly tight, management policy is much more complex than the simple imposition of direct control. Even under conditions of slavery, absolute authority was more apparent than real (Genovese, 1976). Genovese shows that despite the legal fiction that the slave was the master's property, the relationship between them was antagonistic and contradictory rather than unreservedly autocratic. Masters seeking high productivity had to elicit, to a certain extent, the co-operation of the slave. Hence, the growth of 'understandings' and 'customs' about the nature of work.

The connection with firms under capitalism is quite clear - consent needs to be negotiated, even within a direct control framework. Direct control can contain significant internal variations and should not be equated with a total absence of worker discretion. Management may well pursue a policy of dividing workers by granting concessions to key groups while being concerned with a need to be fair. Control here often involves a complex interplay of discipline, paternalism and interest in workers as individuals (Edwards, 1986).

The ostensible passivity on the part of workers in Rainnie's investigation could, of course, be genuine, or it could be a limitation in the research design, that is, the neglect of workers' capacity to exercise discretion. Either explanation, however, seems curious given Rainnie's acceptance of the contradictory nature of the employment relationship and the importance that is accorded to 'labour's varying response' in understanding the labour process. There is no real explanation of how consent is secured, save for brief reference to management stressing a " family atmosphere approach " (p124). This is in sharp contrast to the elucidation of legitimising principles used by management to secure consent and the intricate means of worker struggle and accommodation identified in the Armstrong et al. study in a setting where management undoubtedly had the whip hand (although this firm was much larger than those investigated by Rainnie).

Comprehending the processes involved in the negotiation of order is then crucial to developing a clearer understanding of the texture of workplace relations. There is precious little evidence of this kind within existing accounts of the West Midlands clothing industry and similar firms. Although these issues have been addressed to a certain extent in some studies of the garment industry, they have tended to be in larger firms where the ethnic dimension has been missing. The recent upsurge of interest in industrial relations in small firms has rendered the industrial harmony thesis problematic. However, there has been a tendency, exemplified by Rainnie, to suggest that managerial autocracy is pervasive, especially in the clothing industry. How, then, does management actually manage in such arenas ?

Management

The second major issue is the place of management, how it organises the workplace and how it handles the variety of pressures that it faces. How does management in the West Midlands clothing industry actually manage at the level of the workplace? From profiles of the sector and the recent debates on industrial relations in small firms, the answer appears to be 'ruthlessly and rationally'. For example, an oft-expressed view is that the viability of such concerns rests upon the employment of relatives and community members, both as managers and operatives, at reduced rates (Mars and Ward, 1984). Ward and Smith, for example, found that a common feature of Asian-owned knitwear firms in Leicester was the intensive use of family members in the management of the business (1987: 17).

In the West Midlands, a considerable proportion of the industry's output comes from the labour of women working at home or in small 'sweatshops' (Phizacklea, 1987). Mitter (1985) has outlined the stark exploitation of homeworkers generally and points out that the intensive use of female labour is the cornerstone of the burgeoning of the ethnic economy. Phizacklea, referring to the West Midlands clothing industry, contends that the viability of the sector rests upon the payment of very low wages, long hours, and, in many cases, the evasion of statutory employment duties such as the payment of national insurance contributions (1987: 231).

The intensive use of family and community labour in such concerns and its portrayal as a boon to competitiveness is, then, fairly well documented. Its utility in this respect cannot be doubted - 'family' labour is cheap and the 'problem' of supervision is made easier. However, it is doubtful whether the management of such workplaces, or indeed any workplace, is so rational and control so simple. This point relates fundamentally to the way in which management is conceptualised.

An important theme of the study is how management actually secures consent on the shopfloor. The view that it is achieved through deliberate management strategy has, of course, been a much debated issue. For Braverman, management's imperative was to deskill; R. Edwards (1979) has advanced a three stage approach of management control, that is, the simple-technical-bureaucratic model; Friedman (1977) argues that management has a continuum that ranges from 'responsible autonomy' to 'direct control'. In relation to the clothing industry, Rainnie's suggestion of autocracy has already been noted.

However, by emphasising the negotiation of order, the uncertain trajectory of workplace relations and the significance of informality, the notion of a coherent strategy on the part of management is bound to be problematic. It is doubtful whether firms have explicit well-defined strategies of management control. Rather they will respond to situations in a pragmatic, often ad hoc way. There are likely to be a variety of means of controlling labour and securing commitment, and this will rarely conform to an ideal type, even if the firm does have clear policies (Edwards, 1986).

Control, then, should not be seen as a simple managerial imposition, but the product of a number of different influences. There are many ways in which control can be secured, ranging from close supervision to the favourable treatment of key workers; and they can be present in the same firm. Systems of control emerge from the complexities of managerial practices and worker activity. Control typologies are rarely sensitive to this, suggesting that particular strategies are devised and implemented, whereas control is diverse and complex and the result of past struggles within the social relations of work.

This view is at variance with the treatment of management as a homogeneous grouping without inconsistencies and as rational agents of capital. An approach that appreciates the complexities inherent within management would, as Hyman (1987) argues, need to accept the centrality of the concept of contradiction. Strategic choice is present, not necessarily because of the weakness of structural forces, but because the forces arc themselves contradictory. It is impossible to harmonise the different functions of capital, there being no one best way of managing these contradictions, only 'different routes to partial failure'. Management strategy can therefore best be understood as the programmatic choice among alternatives none of which can prove satisfactory. On this basis, it is necessary to look at the contradictory pressures that management is subjected to in order to fully understand the nature of control in organisations.

Within this framework a number of points are evident. Firstly, management's sole aim is not necessarily the control of the labour process, although to privilege another concern of management, as Rainnie does in relation to competition, is equally inappropriate. Secondly, the notion of management as an all-knowing, all-powerful entity is fundamentally flawed. The contradictory nature of the relationship between capital and labour, and of capital itself, will inevitably result in tensions that have to be managed. Finally, such tensions will be managed in a variety of ways which may have unintended consequences, not some prescribed strategic route.

The intention of the current study is not necessarily to dwell on this level of analysis. After all, the essential point that there is room for action but within a material context has been made convincingly by Hyman, Edwards and others. Rather, the analytical task is to establish the ways in which the contradictory pressures facing management are actually managed at the level of the workplace. In other words, the concern here is with the observation of 'tension management in action' (Newby, 1977a: 423).

The issue of managing conflicting pressures has been a feature of recent studies of management, but these studies have again usually been in large firms (Armstrong, 1986; Smith et al; 1990). The subject that appears to attract most attention in such studies seems to be the extent to which management has goals different from those of the organisation. In their concern to tackle the notion that management is a rational, monolithic and unified force, such studies tend to concentrate upon the importance of inter-management competition and inter-professional rivalry in shaping overall management policy. For example, Smith et al's study of Cadbury charts the tensions that existed between maintaining the personnel aspects of 'Cadburyism' and the increasing unease over the permissive management of industrial relations during the upheavals of the 1970s. The eventual outcome was conditioned by the relative strengths of the functions of management. In his study, Armstrong (1986) examined how the professions of accounting, engineering and personnel attempted to impose their own logics upon the nature of work relations.

Such issues are of undoubted importance in moulding the character of the workplace. The outcome of battles between and within management will have implications for the shopfloor, but of equal significance are the complex processes at the interface between labour and capital. Rather than focusing on what are essentially problems of bureaucracy and intra-management politics, the current study concentrates mainly on the capital-labour relation. In doing so, it focuses more on the essence of management itself than the internal dynamics of management. There is very little scope for intra-management rivalry in small firms of the kind found in West Midlands clothing industry. Yet the contradictions and tensions involved in the management of labour are many and varied.

Conceptually, this level of analysis requires a focus on 'struggle' around the 'frontier of control'. Struggle involves the activities of employers and workers and is a dynamic process that mediates effects from outside the workplace and develops understandings about how work is to be performed. The frontier of control summarises the understandings around issues relating to social relations at work like work allocation, the setting of the piece-rate and so on. It is not a static process - it represents the results of past struggles and its direction cannot necessarily be predicted or prescribed (Edwards, 1990: 129).

The generally unfettered nature of managerial autocracy ascribed to the garment industry per se and clothing firms like those found in the West Midlands in particular reveal little of the nature of such struggles and the concrete ways in which management comes to terms with the tensions and pressures confronting them. There is little empirical coverage of forces that inhibit or constrain management 'rationality' and the complex ways in which employers respond to uncertainty. A rare and partial example is provided by Ward, who found that in one knitwear firm in Leicester "it was better to keep down labour rates and have lots of waste than to pay a good knitter and have more efficient production " (1987: 11). Furthermore, the highly qualified sons in that firm had to remain in subsidiary roles in what was clearly their father's business.

Evidence of this kind, albeit on a anecdotal and sketchy basis, points to the irrationality, or at least 'bounded rationality', of management in minority firms. It gives an indication of the complex nature of management and the importance of contextual features in understanding the actual process of management. Management activity may not be 'rational' on a strictly economic calculation, but seen in the light of managing internal and external relations, it becomes comprehensible. The extent to which such actions are without logic or rational within constraints needs to be explored in much more detail in order to understand the dynamics of workplace relations in such firms and management's role in shaping them.

Ethnicity

The nature of ethnicity and its significance for workplace relations is the third major concern of this study given the preponderance of Asian entrepreneurs and labour within West Midlands clothing sector. The main issue under consideration is the way in which ethnicity influences what happens on the shopfloor. In examining this question, it is important to have a conception of the various facets of ethnicity, namely, racism and culture, and how ethnicity itself connects with gender. It is then necessary to assess the extent to which ethnicity overrides or is subordinate to the unique dynamics of the workplace. In other words, examining ethnicity at work will have important implications for the independence, or otherwise, of the labour process.

In helping to shed light on this question, the labour process literature is of limited utility. The burgeoning contributions to the labour process literature have embraced a variety of issues ranging from subjectivity (Knights, 1990) to the role of the state (Strinati, 1990). Such diversity is to be appreciated since it adds to the richness of the debate. It is, therefore, all the more surprising that ethnicity has barely been mentioned, though the impact of gender, with which it tends to get bundled, has been the subject of increasing, and welcome, attention (see Knights and Wilmott, 1986).

The various studies and discussions on minority firms are more useful in that they demonstrate the multi-layered nature of ethnicity and provide useful contextual evidence of how minority enterprise comes into being and the particular source of its competitive advantage. Three themes are particularly prominent: the context of racism, the 'resourcefulness' of ethnic groups and the gendered nature of ethnicity. Although there have been attempts to integrate these elements (Phizacklea, 1990, Westwood and Bhachu [1988]), rarely have such accounts demonstrated the significance of ethnicity at the level of the workplace.

It would be difficult to grasp the significance of ethnicity without recognising the backdrop of racism. The growth of minority enterprise has been widely debated (Ward and Jenkins, 1984). Ethnic groups have turned to self-employment in increasing numbers, and although there are various explanations of the rise of ethnic business, there can be little doubt that 'the opportunity structure outweighs any cultural predisposition towards entrepreneurship' (Aldrich et al, 1984:205).

In order to combat racial disadvantage, many immigrants have turned to the 'rag' trade, which has traditionally been labour intensive and required little capital or expertise. Asians in the West Midlands and Manchester (Werbner, 1984), and Cypriots in the East End of London (Anthias, 1983) have been prepared to take over the jobs left by white workers and employers and tolerate low wages and poor conditions in order to survive. Hence, rather than having a cultural flair for enterprise, it seemed that minority groups have been sucked into this sector through the limitation of real choices.

Jones's (1992) account of the constraints facing Asian entrepreneurs and labour is a useful illustration of the importance of the context of racism in shaping the fortunes of ethnic enterprise. Although Jones concentrates on Asian retailers in Bradford, his findings apply to much of ethnic enterprise. Jones identifies three sets of constraints that inhibit the development of ethnic business. Firstly, many small firms (and most ethnic businesses are small [Boissevain, 1984]) are in a dependent relationship with large firms, which puts them in an extremely vulnerable position and constrains their potential for growth. Secondly, Asians find themselves starting and being employed in such firms because of the pervasiveness of racism rather than any innate entrepreneurial disposition. Thirdly, minority firms face further discrimination from lending institutions, estate agents and other intermediaries necessary for business growth. When these factors are taken together, it is clear that racism in its various guises plays an important part in shaping the (mis)fortunes of ethnic enterprise.

Such accounts of minority enterprise seek to explain ethnic involvement in the small business sector. In identifying the constraints that racism imposes on such firms, they provide a useful insight into the way minority enterprise is boxed in. What is less well known is how ethnicity actually intervenes on the shopfloor.

The 'ethnicity as a resource' approach (see, for example, Wallman, 1979), which is the second theme, concentrates on the activity of minority groups rather than the impact of racism. It emphasises the ways in which ethnic ties can be used as a resource and regards them as a major spur to enterprise. Typical of studies in this tradition is that of Werbner (1984), which suggests that 'trust', kinship ties, ethnic solidarity and the 'family' were vital to the success of Pakistani entrepreneurs in Manchester.

The final theme gets behind the 'ethnicity as a resource' approach and exposes the gendered nature of ethnicity. This view critically examines the notion of 'family' labour and points up the patriarchal nature of familial ideology. Phizacklea (1990: 77), makes the point that the real resource for ethnic enterprise is not so much the 'family' but the pool of cheap labour supplied by minority women. The patriarchal basis of ethnicity is further highlighted by Mitter (1985), Hoel (1982), and Anthias (1983).

Mitter contends that ethnic and familial links help to keep wages low, and suggests that the ideology of the extended family among Asians makes it easy to enlist a docile, cheap and largely female labour force. Hoel's study further highlights the importance of ethnicity. She argues that the relationship of subservience, servility and passivity that was evident between husband and wife or mother-in-law and daughter-in-law was reproduced to an important extent in the workplace. Moreover, the relationship between employer and worker was underpinned by the conventional relationship between man and woman in the Asian community, but the pattern of control was further complicated by the way in which control in the factory was often exercised via the employer's wife or close female relatives.

Anthias is also concerned with the interplay of 'race', ethnicity and gender. She shows how ethnicity and sexual divisions are used by Greek-Cypriot men to manage disadvantage. Migrant men, in an effort to combat this disadvantage, often turn to small-scale entrepreneurial activity, one of the primary reasons being the opportunity that exists to exploit migrant women. Indeed, in this case, the labour of the migrant women proved to be the cornerstone of the Greek-Cypriot economy.

The intensive use of female labour is underpinned by an ideology that stresses the importance of family and the community. The patriarchal relations that are so much a feature of this community extend to the sphere of work, and in doing so, heavily influence the shape of work relations. The actual manipulation of the labour force involves an assertion of shared class interests, which is possible on the basis of shared ethnic loyalty and honour. Hence, ethnicity is used to obscure the exploitative nature of the capital-labour relationship.

Hoel and Anthias demonstrate that ethnicity is indeed a resource, but it is a resource primarily for migrant men. In supplying evidence of the exploitation of minority women, they confirm Phizacklea's claim regarding the 'gender-blind' nature of much of the ethnic business literature. Yet this concentration on the exploitation of minority women has tended to underplay the extent to which women can use ethnicity for their own ends. In short, a concentration on exploitation runs the risk of minimising the culturally specific resources that women can draw upon to mould their working lives. Wilson (1976) and Parmar (1982) have highlighted instances of Asian women involved in 'resistance' whilst Westwood and Bhachu (1988) have noted the growing activity of minority women. However, there seems to little concrete evidence of the multi-faceted nature of ethnicity and its potential as a resource for women as well as men.

This scenario is mirrored to a significant degree in the more explicitly feminist studies of the workplace, for example, by Westwood (1984), Pollert (1981) and Cavendish (1982). They vividly expose the way in which gender relations operate to the disadvantage of women at work and point up the acute sexual division of labour at the workplace. The generally coercive nature of the workplace is shown to be compounded by the impact of patriarchy.

However, unlike many accounts of minority enterprise, the feminist studies illustrate that women were not totally passive in the face employer subordination. There were instances of distinctly female modes of resistance, which Westwood's study of StitchCo features quite extensively. Women workers there joked with or mocked supervisors, thereby alleviating the degree of subordination that they were subjected to. It seemed that the passivity of women workers was interspersed with sporadic bouts of anger over apparently minor issues. This anger was often spontaneous and unfocused. Another particular characteristic of women's resistance was minor rule-breaking, for example, smoking in the toilets and using factory material to produce goods for friends and relatives. In common with the study by Pollert (1981), Westwood found that the ideology of marriage was further used by younger women as an escape and as a means of coping with the drudgery of work, even though, as the older women proved, the escape was often illusory.

Successful though such studies are in highlighting how women as a collectivity 'resisted' management, there is little evidence of how ethnicity is used as a resource for women despite the fact that, in the Westwood study at least, there were a significant proportion of Asian women workers (although there has been a recent, if partial, attempt to this end [Westwood and Bhachu, 1988]). The ways in which minority women could use their cultural resources to shape their working environment was not explored in any great detail.

What then is the significance of ethnicity on the shopfloor ? Will it, as Burawoy (1979: 201) suggests, be of minimal importance in comparison with what happens inside the labour process or will it have a central role in shaping workplace relations, as Thompson (1983: 81) asserts in relation to gender ? Is there some way of acknowledging the importance of ethnicity without, at the same time, losing sight of the distinctive features of the labour process ? These are issues that need to be addressed in order to establish the significance of ethnicity at work.

Conclusion and Plan of Book

This study sets out to examine the nature of workplace relations in small clothing firms in the West Midlands against the background of the harmony and autocracy views of small firms. Existing studies of clothing firms have provided valuable insights into the character of work relations, but have paid insufficient regard to the processes involved in the negotiation of order, the role of management and the impact of ethnicity at the workplace. These features are of crucial importance to an understanding of the dynamics of workplace relations in the West Midlands clothing sector. In developing the arguments for these particular lines of enquiry, the contributions and limitations of the existing accounts of clothing firms were discussed.

The concept of the negotiation of order signifies a concern with the concrete activities and formal and informal bargaining on the shopfloor. There has been little substantive analysis of how the negotiation of order has been established within the West Midlands clothing industry. In studies of larger firms in the garment sector, the concept has had some coverage indicating that management is usually in the ascendent. Within workplace studies of smaller firms, the once prominent 'industrial harmony' thesis has been rendered problematic, but in its place, seems to be the view that industrial relations are coercive, especially in the clothing industry.

Valuable though the exposure of coercion at the workplace is, the fluid, complex and contested nature of life on the shopfloor fails to come through sufficiently in many of the cases. For example, the many uncertainties and contradictions that are embedded within systems of production were not really explored. In short, the processual aspects of the negotiation of order have not been adequately established.

The second theme of the study, namely the management of workplace relations, has at best received limited coverage. The debate on industrial relations in small firms and the sketchy profiles of the West Midlands clothing industry again suggest that managerial autocracy is the dominant characteristic of shopfloor regimes. That this view is partial is explained by the way management is conceptualised.

In considering how management actually manages labour, the linear view offered by Braverman and the typologies of Friedman and R. Edwards were rendered problematic because they were not sufficiently sensitive to the complex and fluid nature of shopfloor relations. An approach that is sensitive to such complexities would need, as Hyman argues, to accord primacy to the concept of contradiction. Management cannot harmonise the different functions of capital since they are themselves contradictory. All that it can hope to do is to manage the tensions stemming from such conflicting pressures. This 'tension management' has not been adequately addressed in studies of clothing firms and ethnic enterprise.

In relation to ethnicity, three major points emerge from the studies of minority firms. Firstly, the context of racism is vital to an understanding of the growth of the ethnic business sector. Secondly, the 'resourcefulness' of minorities in using ethnicity to overcome discrimination. Thirdly, the gendered nature of ethnicity - insofar as ethnicity is a resource, it is a resource for minority men. What is less well understood is the multi-faceted nature of ethnicity, that is, its ability to obstruct as well as well facilitate managerial autocracy, and the precise impact of ethnicity on the labour process (an issue curiously neglected in the labour process debate).

How are the deficiencies identified in relation to the negotiation of order, management and ethnicity to be tackled ? The plan of the book adumbrates the way in which the issues are to be addressed in the context of the West Midlands clothing industry.

Chapter two examines the way in which the research was actually conducted. It indicates how the methodology facilitated observation of the particular processes at play on the shopfloor and emphasises the importance of my own background.

Chapter three focuses on the nature of management organisation in the West Midlands clothing sector and the ways in which management accommodates the pressures that surround it. The 'rationality' of features like casualisation and the intensive utilisation of 'family' labour in management is questioned in the light of the case study evidence.

Chapter four explores in detail the manner in which the shopfloor was organised and the tensions stemming from the system of production. Accordingly, it looks closely at the processes of recruitment, training, the division of labour, work allocation and the actual operation of the productive system.

Chapter five considers issues around the effort bargain, namely, the rate-fixing process, the nature of supervision and the pace of work. The complex and negotiated nature of the shopfloor and the uncertainties that it generates, are subjected to examination here.

Chapter six assesses the role of ethnicity at the level of the workplace and in doing so, highlights its close connection with gender. The prevailing perspectives on the nature of ethnicity are evaluated in attempting to clarify the impact of ethnicity on workplace relations.

The concluding chapter reflects on the major findings of this study and assesses its wider implications. The question of where the current study fits in relation to others, especially those of Rainnie and Westwood, is considered. Furthermore, in contemplating the extent to which the findings can be generalised, an attempt is made to locate the study in a more general framework of industrial relations. The framework indicates why this study is likely to be typical of the workplace in very small firms and suggests why the nature of social relations at work in Rainnie's setting and other studies in larger firms may have been different.

2

Methodology

This chapter recounts the ways in which the study was conducted. At one level, this task is fairly straightforward. The data were obtained in two stages. The first stage consisted of semi-structured interviews with sixteen owner-managers, the purpose of which was to get a 'feel' for the problems facing such employers. The second stage primarily involved observational fieldwork in three clothing firms (companies A, B and C) over a four month period, followed by regular weekly visits for a year. Although an accurate presentation of the research design and chronology, this description depicts an exceedingly sterile rendition of the actual research process. The way in which the study was conducted did not follow some goal-directed, linear path. As Bell and Newby (1977) and Bryman (1989) have pointed out, the actual process of research often deviates from the prescribed and brittle formulae contained in conventional approaches to research. Yet accounts of actual and 'messy' research are probably more useful than pristine prescriptions, for they provide valuable insights into a range of real issues that researchers face in the field and different ways in which they can be addressed. Accordingly, this chapter catalogues the way in which the research was actually carried out.

After a brief introduction to the three case study companies, the discussion begins by illustrating the extent to which my family and I have been immersed in the clothing industry. The study is not simply a product of a survey and a few months in the field - it is a testimony to the many years in which our fortunes have rested on the survival of the family business. This is followed by a consideration of some fieldwork issues that were salient to the study. Some of the problems of earlier surveys on the

West Midlands clothing industry, notably around the issue of access, are examined together with the ways in which the survey for the current study was able to avoid these pitfalls. Access to employers was made possible by the 'trust' that I was able to achieve - a trust that relied crucially on family and community connections. The basis of this trust is considered along with the connections that enabled me to get into the firms and tap into the workplace culture.

The market position of the case study companies is covered in the next chapter when considering the structure of the West Midlands clothing industry. However, a brief description of the firms is provided here to set the scene. Company A came into being in 1979. It is one part of the family business, the other elements being a wholesale operation (run by Bas, my younger brother) and a separate clothing manufacturing company (run by my elder brother, Sol, and a cousin). Phu (my father), who runs company A, employs around fifteen direct workers all of whom are male. There are five machinists, two cutters and ancillary staff. It is quite unusual for clothing firms in the West Midlands to employ male machinists exclusively; but this situation was a product of circumstance rather than design. The firm had tried to enlist female machinists but none were prepared to travel to the rather isolated premises where company A was located.

The overwhelming majority of the company's production comes from outworkers and sub-contractors. They account for over 80% of the firm's output. Some of these external workers are situated in premises adjacent to the proprietor's home, which are supervised by the proprietor's two daughters-in-law.

Company B is run by two brothers and a cousin. The company employs around twenty-five machinists on the premises who produce the bulk of the firm's output. In addition to these on-site machinists, the company utilises a small number of outworkers and sub-contractors. As well as the machinists and the three partners (who between them share the cutting duties), the company has on its staff three packers and one supervisor.

Company C is run by nine brothers and the wives of four of them. Between them, they are responsible for managing, cutting, quality control and supervision. The company employs around thirty machinists on the premises, the majority of whom have been working for the firm for over ten years. In addition to these on-site workers, the company makes use of homeworkers and sub-contractors, especially during the busy season.

The Family Business

Nature and Origins

" ... full time research is not a job: it is a way of life, and so one's life becomes woven into the research just as much as research becomes part of one's life " (Moore, 1977: 87).

For two years, Moore 'ate, breathed and slept' Sparkbrook in order to unravel the processes of racism in an inner city area in Birmingham. I have been in and around the clothing industry for slightly longer. For most of my life I have been involved with the clothing trade. More accurately, I have been privy to a particular part of the 'rag trade'. It has not been a world of cat walks, designers, models and other such features associated with the world of high fashion. Rather, it has been an existence of hard labour in a harsh and hostile environment. For my family and, to a lesser extent, myself, long tedious hours in the factory of doing almost everything from clipping loose threads from jackets to trying to extract payment for goods from boorish wholesalers in the East End of London have been the natural order of things. The family business has been just that - a family business, with no real dividing line between the home and the factory. Every member of my family is firmly ensconced in the clothing industry. My father is the head of the whole enterprise, although most of his time is spent running company A. My mother is not 'officially' involved in any part of the business, but at an informal level her influence is considerable. She recruits machinists, mediates in disputes between workers and management and plays an active role 'behind the scenes' in managing the company's financial resources. My two elder sisters and one younger sister are married into clothing families, where they work as sewing machinists and assist in the management of the in-laws' firms. My elder brother runs a clothing manufacturing business with a cousin. This business was 'created' especially for him by my father. My younger brother is in charge of the family - owned warehouse. Furthermore, beyond the immediate family, numerous relatives are engaged in varying capacities in the local clothing industry.

Yet, it was not always like this. My father came to England from India in the late 1950s leaving his wife and two young daughters behind. Like many others in his position, he did not have much in the way of possessions and had no job. Finding cramped accommodation with other newly arrived Indians, he eventually started work in a foundry. He laboured hard in order to save enough money to bring his family over, who arrived some five years later. He saved hard so that he could scrape enough money together to escape from the toil of factory work and start a business. He duly opened a grocery shop in the early 1970s, but soon disposed of this in order to set up a clothing factory in partnership with two cousins. This business survived until 1979 when the various partners decided to go their different ways. It was in 1979 that company A came into being, followed a few years later by the family warehouse and the clothing business for my elder brother.

Personal History

My own personal involvement in the 'family business' has been extensive but more variable than other family members. For me, life revolved around the family, the business and education. And it continues to do so. As a student, I recall writing essays in the shop, postponing a tutorial because I had to make a delivery of garments and ruminating on academic debates whilst engaged in delivering and collecting work from the homes of outworkers. Today, the emphasis may have shifted a touch, but the juxtaposition remains. Part of this study was written up on the premises of company A. Indeed during the fieldwork period, my father went on holiday to India leaving my younger brother and me to run the firm.

Between 1984 and 1986, the balance of interests appeared to shift quite markedly in the direction of the 'business'. I started to work full-time in company A. It was envisaged that I would remain there permanently, eventually replacing my father at the helm. During that two year period, I was exposed to the extreme tedium of 'managing' a clothing factory. I performed a number of functions, from the actual cutting of garments to negotiating deals with customers. The trials of working long hours, coping with the competing demands of wholesalers, workers, officialdom and the family finally prompted me to leave. This was an extremely difficult decision since I was effectively removing myself from a 'natural' path laid down for me by my family.

I 'escaped' into higher education only to return to the clothing industry a year later, although in a different guise. In 1987 I undertook a project on behalf of Wolverhampton Council on the training needs of the clothing industry in the Wolverhampton area (Wolverhampton District Council, 1988; Ram, 1988). The project involved interviewing over thirty manufacturers, the overwhelming majority of whom were Asian, in order to establish their training requirements. The outcome of this project was the creation of a clothing centre for the training of sewing operatives. I was the first manager of that centre, and as manager I liaised closely with local employers as well as potential recruits to the industry. I left that post in 1989 in order to enter the world of academe, and embarked upon the current research towards the end of that year.

Researching the Current Study

Previous Surveys

Before discussing the survey stage of the study, it might be useful to relate the experiences of previous survey work undertaken in the area. The first major survey was produced in 1983 by Leigh and North. It was a general profile of the West Midlands clothing sector. Although it contained much useful information on the scale of the local industry and its most pressing problems, much of its information was derived from 'key informants' in the comparatively few large companies in the area and training bodies. There was very little evidence on the small firms that make up the bulk of the sector in the region.

Getting into clothing companies in the West Midlands is notoriously difficult. It is not uncommon for researchers looking for the most basic data to be refused admission to the premises, let alone reaching the stage of asking questions. This has usually been put down to a 'distrust' of authority and a fear of officialdom, notably the Inland Revenue. These fears are not to be understated. On one occasion a few years ago, whilst working temporarily in my brother's clothing firm in Smethwick, I witnessed someone being refused admission to the premises on three separate occasions. My cousin, who was in charge of the business in my brother's absence on holiday, did not know who the man at the door was, and feared the worst. He wore a suit and carried a briefcase, which seemed to add up to a very formal demeanour. It later transpired that the person in question was a vending machine salesman.

It is not so much that manufacturers have something to hide. Rather, it appears to be a fear of the unknown. Most manufacturers employ Asian labour, they buy raw material from Asian suppliers and sell their goods to Asian wholesalers. The white world is not normally an important part of this trading network. Where it does figure, it is usually in the form of demands for taxes, social security queries and other information relating to the operation of the business. Given this situation, it is hardly surprising that researchers seeking detailed information will be given a fairly indifferent welcome.

In 1984, a very rudimentary survey was carried out in order to establish a profile of the clothing industry in the Birmingham area (Handsworth Technical College, 1984). The survey was bedevilled with problems of access, despite the fact that the white researcher who undertook the study claimed to have been 'accepted' by the community. In 1988, a larger survey examining the training needs of the clothing industry in Birmingham experienced similar problems (Lewis, 1988). The two researchers involved in this survey, one white and one Afro-Caribbean, were refused access to quite a number of firms despite the fact that they sought fairly basic data.

In a similar survey that I undertook for Wolverhampton District Council in the same year, securing access did not prove problematic. I believe that my ethnic origin and experience of the clothing industry were major reasons for the relatively trouble-free process of gaining access. Even though the type of information required was fairly rudimentary, 'trust' was important, and it seemed that my background greatly facilitated the attainment of such trust. In return for the information, I was prepared to listen to the employers' grievances and any questions they put to me. Quite a few wanted to know about my family. Some manufacturers sought advice on how to get a grant from the council or any other financial pickings that the council may have been offering. One manufacturer sought a more practical and immediate price - he would only grant me an interview if I helped him to tie his turban.

The Survey Stage

The survey stage of the current study comprised interviews with sixteen employers in Birmingham, Sandwell and Wolverhampton. The companies were chosen because they were 'typical' in the sense that they depicted many of the features characteristic of clothing firms in the West Midlands. For example, they were Asian-owned, they employed fewer than thirty people and they were not particularly advanced technologically. In order to gain an impression of the diversity of the West Midlands clothing firms, it was also important however to visit different types of firm. Hence, it was necessary to cover employers engaged in different sectors of the market. This requirement prompted the interview of manufacturers producing on a Cut Make and Trim basis ([CMT] - this is where the company simply makes to order for a larger manufacturer, there is no direct contact with the eventual customer), firms supplying wholesalers and manufacturers selling directly to retailers.

Gaining access to such firms was not a straightforward process. It was not simply a matter of looking up manufacturers in the appropriate business directory and pleading for an interview. Despite my background, busy employers in the cut-throat world of clothing would probably regard spending two hours answering fairly searching questions posed by a researcher as perhaps not the most productive use of their time. Moreover, I did not want the questions answered in a perfunctory manner - I wanted them to be prepared to elaborate and wax at their leisure about the pleasures and pitfalls of life as a clothing manufacturer.

Access and Trust

In order to have any hope of eliciting these types of responses, I had to rely on 'trust'. I had to rely on my own resources to establish contact with such firms. In drawing on my own resources, I used an 'opportunistic' approach, recommended by many (Bresnen, 1988; Buchannan et al, 1988; Crompton and Jones, 1988), in which contacts, friends and relatives were used to the full. Being a member of a 'respected' family in the local Asian community was an undoubted advantage. Pettigrew (1981), a white woman married into a Sikh family, has remarked on the usefulness of family connections in eliciting information for her research into state-level politics in rural India. Being part of a prominent family allowed her access to individuals and organisations which she would not have been privy to without such connections. Similarly, my family's connections smoothed my entry into many Asian firms. Some employers felt 'honour-bound' to talk to me. However, in order to get the spread of companies that I required, I had to go through intermediaries. I asked employers whom I was familiar with to introduce me to such firms. On one occasion, the introduction was made over the telephone in my presence by an employer acquaintance of mine, " I've got a friend who's writing a book about manufacturers. It's okay, he's one of us. He wants to come and see you - have a chat with him."

The actual issues raised with employers related to the reasons for setting up the business, their position in the market, competition, work allocation, external labour, payment systems, recruitment and training. Once employers started talking to me, they would often go on at length to describe the difficulties of managing a clothing company, often relating examples to illustrate the point. One employer commenting on the so called' labour shortage' claimed that 'Young Asian girls aren't interested in working in a factory no more - they're lazy. They'd rather work in shops or offices where they can talk to friends'. Another spoke of the racism of chainstore buyers, 'I took this jacket to.... The buyer made me wait more than an hour before letting me see him, and then he did not want the jacket. I gave the jacket to a white agent. He took it to the same buyer and got the order'. Some employers bemoaned the proliferation of 'cowboys starting up in their own front rooms', while others spoke of the difficulties of keeping apace with the rapidly changing fashions.

Trust, then, was crucial to the whole process of the survey, and its acquisition was not always down to any personal relationship that I had developed with the employers in question. 'Trust guarantees' were made possible by virtue of belonging to a 'respected' family and the assurances of intermediaries. It was these factors that facilitated the often frank disclosures from the employers questioned.

The Case Studies

If trust was a crucial factor in the survey stage of the study, its centrality to the detailed case study work cannot be over stated. Contacts, friends and relatives pressed into service at the behest of intermediaries might be willing to be subjected to an afternoon's inquisition at the hands of a curious interlocutor - but would they be prepared to endure many months of me generally hanging around and firing questions ? This was an altogether more sensitive proposition. Hoel's less than warming account of Asian clothing manufacturers in Coventry and the popular perception of ruthless 'sweatshop' employers in the West Midlands do not inspire much confidence for this type of study. Yet, if one was to achieve an insight into the complex nature of workplace relations, then it was necessary to witness the processes at play on the shopfloor over a period of time.

The fact that the negotiation of access into the case study firms was relatively problem-free reflected the importance of family connections and my background rather than the employers' belief in the intrinsic merits of my research. In all three companies, community and familial ties were drawn upon in order to effect an entry.

In the case of company B, I had known one of the partners who ran the firm for over fifteen years - he was a school-mate of my brothers. We would socialise together quite regularly. I informed him of the nature of the study and requested access into this firm. He agreed, but it was an agreement made possible by the strength of kinship ties rather than any obvious enthusiasm for the study.

With company C, community ties were again drawn on in order to gain access. My father and the father of the brothers who ran company C were of the same caste and from the same village in India. They had come to this country in similar circumstances and had known each other for over thirty years. To cement this relationship even further, a cousin of mine had married one of the brothers of company C.

In the case of my father's firm, company A, gaining access was even less problematic. I had worked for the company, either full-time or part-time, since it came into being and, in a sense, I have never left. Despite my present occupation, I am still associated with the company. Although I have no formal or legal connection with the firm, I can sign cheques, purchase stock, make use of the firm's equipment and give instructions to the company's workers.

Within company A, my presence over the duration of the fieldwork was not seen as unusual. Workers were accustomed to seeing me writing, asking questions and engaging in conversation. In the past, whilst working there, I was usually involved in part-time or full-time study. Hence the sight of me writing in the office or on the shopfloor was not particularly exceptional. It was accepted that I was 'doing work for college'.

Because I was regarded as 'educated', workers would often ask me to assist with sorting out social security queries, housing issues, passport problems and other such difficulties. These tasks were nothing new, I had regularly performed them whilst working at the factory. During the course of the fieldwork, I helped one of the workers send for his wife stranded in Pakistan because of immigration 'red-tape', I complained to the local authority about delays in the renovation of another worker's house and dealt with a number of social security problems. Furthermore, I was often asked (by employers and workers alike in all three firms) for my advice on the education of their children. A partner in company B wanted me to 'get a place' for his cousin on a law degree. One of the brothers in company C asked me to preach the importance of higher education to his two sons. Whilst making a delivery to a homeworker engaged by company A, the machinist asked me for my opinion on the merits of particular university courses for his daughter.

Tapping into the Shopfloor Culture

Once access had been negotiated and management in the various companies understood that I would be around for some time, there were little if any restrictions on my movements. At no point did management in the case study companies prevent me from talking to anyone or constrain my activities. However, the management's apparent sangfroid should not be overstated, since their general amenability was due to obligation rather comfiture with my presence on the shopfloor.

Although there were no formalities, rules or constraints on my movements on the shopfloor, there was, nevertheless, an informal, unspoken
agreement, the adherence to which permitted me considerable latitude
and discretion. For example, although I did request, and was granted,
formal interviews with management, I kept them to a minimum and used
them mainly to extract factual information. The reasons for this were quite
simple. Firstly, the managers were very busy people. They were continually engaged in one task or another rarely having the opportunity for
decent breaks let alone time to partake in interviews with me. Had I
insisted on formal, structured interviews, it would have been doubtful
that I would have secured the required information and, more to the point,
I may have quickly outstayed my welcome. Secondly, by far the most
interesting insights came from general observations and informal conversations that I struck up with managers while they were engaged in their
daily tasks. I would wait for the most opportune moment and then start
a conversation in order to elicit the required information. The main themes
of these conversations tended to be their relationships with customers, the
role of the family in the firm, the payment system, the management of the
machinists and generally what life was like as an Asian garment manufacturer. My reliance on informality minimised my obtrusiveness to such an
extent that, after a week or so, my presence barely caused comment.

Despite the extreme industry of many of the managers, once they
engaged in conversation with me they would often take the opportunity
to vent their feelings and talk about almost anything. For example, Gel,
one of the brothers who ran company C, always appeared to be busy. He
would be immersed in such diverse tasks as fixing machines, creating a
new design, producing a jacket sample, setting a piece-rate and dealing
with customers. I had very few formal interviews with him and when we
were engaged in such a process, I was careful not to detain him unduly.
Yet it was not uncommon for him to strike up conversations with me in
which he would talk of his general frustrations, the 'problems' with the
machinists and the burden of working for the family. He often spoke of his
desire to leave the 'rut' of the family business and branch out on his own,
perhaps in the field of design. However, the 'pull' of the family was too
great.

Discussions with the other brothers in company C, management in
company B and workers in company A followed a similar pattern and
were equally wide-ranging. Furthermore, the discussions and conversations were precisely that - they involved me as well as the respondents
answering questions and relating my experiences . Many of them, for

instance, experienced a certain exasperation at my current occupation. They could not understand that watching them and talking to them was part of my job. 'How was it that I got paid for watching them work ?' was the general basis of their incredulity, To a certain extent, I shared their disbelief. Having done their job, inhabiting the world of academia seems little like 'real' work. Nevertheless, I tried to respond to their questions honestly and in a natural manner.

There were also many questions about my family, which was not surprising given our familial and community connections. Rarely, if ever did I adopt the role of a 'textbook' interviewing which exhorts the interviewer to remain aloof while seeking to extract information from the respondent. It would have been totally absurd and counter-productive if I had attempted to remain indifferent to questions from people I had known for many years. The utility of this exchange process in the field has been remarked on by others. Oakley, for example, makes the point that finding out about people through interviewing is best achieved when the interviewer is prepared to invest his or her own personal identity in the relationship (1981:41).

The comparative ease with which conversations developed, my relative unobtrusiveness and the speed with which I was generally accepted in the workplace owed much to my background. My background was crucial in enabling me to understand and appreciate the unwritten rules of shopfloor culture. I was from a 'respected' family, I was Asian, I knew the manufacturing industry and knew how companies like these worked. These resources were instrumental in my acceptance in these firms. They sensitised me to the daily ebb and flow of factory life enabling me to judge when was the right moment to intervene and when I should hold back.

Bulmer (1988) makes the point that language is an important part of the art of fitting into a setting. Being able to speak fluent Punjabi was essential in understanding people at the workplace, but of equal importance was my capacity to be conversant in the language of the particular shopfloor cultures. In order to really unravel complex issues, it is necessary, as Oakley claims to 'get inside the culture'. Commenting on her own research on women and the transition to motherhood, Oakley states that " A feminist interviewing women is both 'inside' the culture and participating in that which she is observing " (1981: 57). Hobbs, an 'EastEnder' researching 'entrepreneurship' and the police in the East End of London, similarly flags up the importance of this point, " I had come to accept that my background, and particularly my London accent were major attributes, and I became more confident of utilising aspects of style, linguistic constructs and any knowledge of the ecology and culture of the East End " (1988: 5). My background enabled me to be an 'insider'. Without this intimate knowledge of the nuances, idiosyncrasies and customs of life on the shopfloor, in the family and within an Asian community attempting to find its way in British society, the task of researching workplace relations in such settings would have been extremely difficult.

Talking to the Women

The primary concern of this study was management, but in order to ascertain the ways in which order was negotiated on the shopfloor, the part played by the machinists (most of whom were women) had to be brought into the picture. Despite my vantage point as an 'insider', researching the machinists was perhaps the most sensitive part of my remit. It was here that the culture had its most obvious impact. The nature of gender relationships in Asian society was a factor that had to be taken into careful consideration in dealings with the machinists. Pettigrew, in relating her experiences of undertaking research in India, pointed out that contact between men and women in the rural setting of the Punjab was highly regulated and had important implications for the family, "Customarily they have not been expected to talk to men except on certain prescribed occasions ... The reputation of the family depends on the behaviour and conduct of its women " (1981: 66). Most of the women in companies B and C were from the Punjab and appeared to display a fairly strong attachment to their culture. In recognition of this, the women worked in separate rooms from the men. Given this setting, it would have been extremely foolish of me to simply engage individual machinists in conversation in the manner that I did with the men in management. Sig, a partner in company B, was only half joking when he said to me " You can talk to the women, but not the young ones. " Again, it was necessary to create a climate of trust with the machinists and display sensitivity towards the cultural norms that most workers here obviously adhered to.

Initially, I asked the supervisors to let the machinists know that I was conducting research into clothing companies. I asked them to relay the confidential nature of the study and that it had absolutely nothing to do with the council or the Department for Social Security. After this was done, I made regular sorties into the machinists' room for a month or so. I did not interview any of the operatives during this time, being content to listen and observe at this stage. This allowed the machinists time to become accustomed to my presence on the shopfloor. Indeed, it was the machinists who asked me questions about the study, about my family and whether or not I was married. Some even recognised me; one asked me to pass on her regards to my sister (it transpired this particular machinist had gone to school with my elder sister).

Through these regular visits to the shopfloor, I gained rich material, but there was still a need for more direct and factual information. I wanted to know why they came to this country, why they chose this industry and this company, how often they had to switch jobs and their general thoughts about life on the shopfloor. To do this I needed to talk to them as individuals, but again it would have been unwise for me to interview them alone. Consequently, I asked a senior machinist in companies B and C to accompany me when I questioned individual operatives. The senior machinist was not necessarily acting as interpreter, for I can converse quite fluently in the machinists' mother tongue (Punjabi). Rather, she was there to act as a chaperone and support.

It appeared to be a fairly productive manoeuvre, for the machinists appeared to be amused rather than intimidated by the interviews. After the interviews, my presence on the shopfloor went virtually unnoticed, save for the continual offers of cups of tea on my arrival. Some of the women referred to me variously as 'son', 'our boy' or a colloquial version of my first name.

Although the data that I gained from my observations and discussions with the women was rich and contained valuable insights, it is perhaps this area that constitutes the main limitation of the study. As an Asian man operating in an environment where Asian women were obviously strongly in accord with their particular customs imported virtually intact from the Punjab, it was impossible for me to participate in the working and domestic lives in the manner that Westwood did with white women workers in StitchCo. (Whether she achieved this degree of congruence with the Asian workers in her study however, is debatable.) It would have been impossible for me to do and extremely foolhardy to try.

However, in mitigation, two points need to be stressed. Firstly, the focus of this study was management rather than the lot of women workers. This was not primarily an ethnographic exercise in the vein of Cavendish, Pollert or Westwood. Secondly, the issues raised in connection with the workforce - for example, the resources that Asian women drew upon to shape their working environment - were apparent and available for analysis. Perhaps the finer details of the culture on the shopfloor could have been painted in more vividly by an Asian woman researcher, but the general processes at play were captured.

Objectivity and Independence

Like other work employing various forms of participant observation, this study potentially lays itself open to a variety of criticisms which, taken together, relate to the supposed 'subjectivity' of this approach (see Burgess, 1984: 82-83). Jenkins for example, makes the point that " ... one negotiates an identity and this identity colours the rest of the research. By its very nature, participant observation must lead to partial accounts " (1984a: 161). Burgess warns of the danger of 'going native' whereby researchers play their roles so well that they are unable to gather data or record observations (1984: 81). Then there is the whole question of generalisability (Bryman, 1989: 172-179).

Important though these points are, their force in relation to the current study can be tempered by highlighting certain features which militated against undue partiality. These features included methodological pluralism, the diversity of my own background, the benefits of being a researcher as well as an 'insider', and a concern for the wider implications of the study. Each will now be considered.

In terms of the actual form of participant observation, I was not a 'covert' or 'full' participant observer in the way, for instance, that Dalton (1959) was. I did not disguise my identity or the purpose of my presence, and I was not constrained by having to assume a full-time work role. My intention was to undertake research, and those around me were aware of that. Rather than being a full participant or a pure observer, I was more a 'participant-as-observer' (Gold, 1952, in Burgess, 1984: 81), a role which essentially involves the researcher developing relationships with key informants. By adopting this method, I was not confined to a particular role or level within the organisation, and I had the freedom to pursue any line of inquiry that I felt would be germane to my investigation.

Moreover, although the participant-as-observer role was crucial to the study, it was not the only research method used. The observational work was complemented by a wide-ranging and intensive survey of sixteen 'typical' clothing manufacturers in the West Midlands. The methodology, therefore, contained a quantitative component too. Furthermore, once on the factory floor, formal and informal discussions were held with workers and managers. While not diluting the potency of the participant-as-observer role, these other approaches afforded a certain methodological heterogeneity which guarded against the problem of partiality that is sometimes seen as a significant drawback of the pure participant observer method (Jenkins, 1984a: 161).

An example from the current study demonstrates the utility of having an eclectic methodology. At the survey stage, all sixteen owner-managers interviewed stated that machinists were individually responsible for the mistakes that they made on a garment, and they were not paid for rectifying them. This was seen as non-contentious and seemed to be taken for granted. However, during the detailed case study investigations, it was evident that this was not the case. Machinists devised a number of ways of getting around being identified as the person responsible for sewing the garment, by not putting their 'tag' on the garment for example. Furthermore, management would not always enforce the rectification of mistakes. It would often depend on whether they could 'get away with it', how urgent the order was and the 'hassle' it would cause if the machinist were to be confronted. Consequently, it was not uncommon to find the supervisor, who was usually paid a wage rather than piece-work, repairing the garment.

This example serves to illustrate the benefits of using a combination of research methods for data collection. A total reliance on survey evidence would not have brought out the complex and contested nature of workplace relations. However, without it, the pervasiveness of the issue might not have been recognised.

The diversity of my personal background was a further defence against undue subjectivity. As I have pointed out my social and familial milieux were a considerable resource and invaluable in affording insights into work relations in West Midlands clothing firms. However, an equally strong theme that has permeated much of my life has been my attachment to education. I have been in higher education as a student and lecturer (or both) since leaving school in 1981. Even whilst working for the family business or other organisations, I was involved in part-time study or part-time lecturing. My areas of academic interest, though, have not often been thought of as central to the world of commerce. Following courses in politics, the processes (as opposed to the prescriptions) of management and industrial relations has not been a particularly common experience amongst typical garment manufacturers in the West Midlands. Indeed, many employers in the sector have not been educated in any formal sense and have responded indifferently to training initiatives (Lewis, 1988).

My academic experiences did not necessarily equip me to become a better functionary within capitalism, but they did inculcate a belief in the virtues of critical analysis. Indeed, it is a belief that is central to my occupation today as a lecturer/ researcher, and it is a belief that informs the current study. Although the focus of the study is management, the intention is not to produce a piece of social reporting chronicling how awful it is to be a manager. This work is not a counterpoint to the studies by Cavendish, Pollert and Westwood, despite the fact that it does contain evidence that suggests the lot of the average employer is pretty dire. Rather, the current study sets out to provide a more systematic analysis of the workplace. Perhaps it could be regarded as a 'thinking manager's' stance, that is, of someone who knows the workings of the industry but is also aware of wider considerations.

The unique combination of my 'insider' status and concern for critical research should then militate against undue subjectivity while, at the same time, allowing for a genuine appreciation of the dynamics of life on the shopfloor. One area where this should be evident is in the discussion of management 'rationality'. The 'rationality' or otherwise of management in this sector is an important theme of the study. For example, a seemingly popular view is that clothing manufacturers in the region survive hostile markets through the intensification and casualisation of work (Mitter, 1985). This appears to be a fairly 'rational' policy on the part of management. However, on closer inspection, the nature of work organisation is demonstrated to be much more complex, uncertain and unpredictable. A pure 'insider's' account may run the risk of 'telling it how it is' without sufficiently questioning the vagaries of workplace behaviour and the existing order. On the other hand, a totally detached investigation may not fully comprehend the dynamics of the processes at play on the shopfloor and therefore may regard the behaviour as aberrant or without logic. As Dalton points out in defence of his 'masquerading research' into the informal aspects of management organisation, 'Studying situations at a distance the investigator may be so "objective" that he misses the subject matter and cannot say what he is objective about' (1959: 283).

My position, however, enables the 'rationality' or 'bounded rationality' of management to be explored and analysed against the context in which it operates. Hopefully, the 'observations together with theoretical insights [will] make seemingly irrational or paradoxical behaviour comprehensible to those within and beyond the situation that is being studied' (Burgess, 1984: 79).

Finally, there is the concern about the generalisabilty of participant observation studies and qualitative research in general. Others have pursued this debate at great length (Bryman, 1988a). In the context of the current study, this issue has been addressed in four ways. Firstly, by the plurality of the research methods mentioned earlier. Secondly, throughout the study, my evidence is compared with others. Thirdly, three companies are studied rather than just that of my family. Furthermore, the study of these three companies allowed coverage of different types of firm (for example, family/ non-family dominance of key management roles and heavy/ marginal reliance on external labour). The nature of these companies, the survey stage and previous work (Ram, 1988) allied to my own extensive experience of the West Midlands clothing sector strongly enhances the 'typicality' of the current study. Finally, the concluding chapter of this study assesses the wider implications of the findings and attempts to locate them within a more general framework of workplace relations.

Conclusion

This chapter has discussed the ways in which the actual process of research was conducted. Rather than outlining the research design in a technical sense, it was considered more valuable to provide an insight into the reality of what happened. To this end, it was important to note the considerable extent to which my family and I have lived, and continue to live with the clothing industry. The fruits of the study are a product of that history, not just my time on the shopfloor of three companies.

The resources available to me by virtue of my family and community connections, together with my experience of 'hands on' management in the rag trade, enabled me to surmount some of the obstacles that hindered previous research efforts in the area. Family and community connections were fully utilised to get 'quality' access into companies at both survey and case study stages. Moreover, it was these resources together with a certain sensitivity deriving from my background that enabled me to access the culture of the shopfloor.

However, despite the considerable advantages of these resources, my attachment to education and familiarity with the traditions of research serves to ensure that the study is more than an exercise in social reporting. Mindful of the problem of excessive partiality, the fluid and eclectic nature of the research process and a concern for the wider implications guarded against undue subjectivity. What follows is a unique combination of an 'insider's' account and considerations from the wider context.

List of Characters

For ease of identification, below is a list of characters who will figure prominently in the current research. Other actors will be referred to, but their identity will be made clear at the appropriate stages in the study.

Company A

Phu - Proprietor (my father)
Gee - Cutter
Fee - Driver/ general assistant
Luk - Machinist

Company B

S - Manager (one of three partners who own and run the firm)
Dor - Supervisor (white female)

Company C

Gel - De facto managing director
Suneta - Sample machinist (also Gel's wife)

3

Management Organisation

This chapter examines the nature of management in the West Midlands clothing industry. It looks at the particular pressures that management face, how they respond to them and the manner in which they endeavour to organise the workplace. The central theme is how management struggles to manage in an uncertain environment. The management of uncertainty has been an issue central to recent debates on management strategy (Ferner, 1985: Hyman, 1987; Kelly, 1985: Streeck, 1987) and is regarded by some as the most important task facing employers. According to Streeck (1987: 211) the central strategic problem that employers face is

'... to find ways of managing an unprecedented degree of economic uncertainty deriving from a need for continuous rapid adjustment to a market environment that seems to have become permanently more turbulent than in the past. Within this increasingly unpredictable environment, management needs to address itself to the task of matching, or achieving a fit between, markets, product range, technology and work organisation'.

Within the orthodox or prescriptive literature on business strategy, this matching process is regarded as unproblematic. Any contradictions between the various functions of management and conflict between labour and capital are ignored or marginalised. As noted earlier, however, the notion of management as some kind of rational and coherent sequence of events is highly problematic. However, equally unsatisfactory was the Braverman-inspired view that management's sole concern was the control of labour through a strategy of deskilling. An approach that appreciates the complexities that confront management, would, as Hyman argues, need to accept the centrality of the concept of contradiction. The scope for choice exists not necessarily because of the weakness of structural forces, but because the forces themselves are contradictory. It is impossible to harmonise the different functions of capital since there is no one best way of managing these contradictions, only different routes to the achievement of limited success. Management strategy can therefore be best understood as the programmatic choice among alternatives, none of which can prove satisfactory.

On this basis, one must look at the range of pressures that management is subjected to in order to better understand the nature of control in organisations. Management's contradictory role as both the co-ordinator of complex productive operations and, at the same time, as a vehicle for discipline, will evolve contradictory responses. It is by examining these responses against this context that the dynamics of labour control can best be understood (Hyman, 1987).

Although Hyman's framework is useful and provides a basis for the examination of the management of labour, the approach is programmatic insofar as it offers a recipe for analysis rather than concrete empirical evidence. Debates centring on the grand question of management strategy have tended to be conducted in this broad manner with comparatively little empirical support. Streeck, for example, claims that employers' attempts to come to terms with their increasingly uncertain environment are hampered by uncertainties within management which stem from the inappropriateness of the industrial relations system (1987: 211). Generally, this might be a valid observation, but the detail upon which it is based seems to be lacking.

Ferner's (1985) analysis of the political constraints facing the management of British Rail during the mid 1980s offers a useful insight into how management responded to a multiplicity of often contradictory objectives. His account of 'flexible rostering' reveals how a particular set of economic and political factors - recession, Conservative government policy towards the public sector and political pressure for a re-definition of the railways' role - interacted with internal pressures on management - notably the cycle of investment, workforce and union demands and the need to ensure staff commitment. The interaction of such conflicting pressures imposed constraints on management's freedom to manoeuvre.

The study by Ferner provides a specific contextual illustration of how management attempted to accommodate a whole range of tensions. In a similar vein, by discussing the nature of management organisation in the West Midlands clothing industry, this chapter aims to provide an insight into the way in which management handles the uncertainties that confront it.

Existing accounts of the clothing industry have tended to neglect the role of management (Westwood, 1984, for example) or make statements of a general kind with little evidence deriving from actual investigation of the workplace. Mitter, for instance, makes the point that much of the industry in this region has survived through the intensive use of ethnic and familial labour (1985: 55). At a broad level, statements of this kind, while not entirely inaccurate, fail to pay sufficient regard to the complex nature of the management process even in small, relatively unsophisticated firms. Management do not do not simply impose 'direct control' over the workforce in order to stay in business. The organisation of the labour process in this particular context is a much more complicated affair shaped by a range of pressures that simultaneously serve to constrain and provide opportunities for management.

The concern here is with the ways in which management endeavours to accommodate the pressures to which they are subject and how they organise production in the light of these pressures. Accordingly, the first of three main sections examines the structure of the West Midlands clothing sector and the problems (particularly those stemming from the market) that it poses for management. The growth of the sector is considered since it is a relatively recent phenomenon and has occurred while more traditional manufacturing industries have declined. This is followed by an analysis of the particular market that local clothing manufacturers operate in and the problems that they face in the areas of training, garment design and the supply of cloth.

Is the uncertainty arising from these pressures managed by autocracy in the form of the casualisation and intensification of labour as many seem to have suggested ? The second section critically examines the notion of casualisation and assesses whether or not it is simply a question of loading and off-loading labour according to the dictates of the market. The final section considers the intensification of work in relation to familial labour and explores the assumed rationality of familial involvement in the management of the firm.

Before embarking on the substantive analysis of the region's clothing sector, it is necessary to undertake a brief appraisal of recent developments in the British clothing industry in order to have an appreciation of the context in which the West Midlands clothing sector operates.

Recent Developments in the United Kingdom Clothing Industry

Since the 1970s, the British clothing industry has been subjected to intense international competition and major shifts in the pattern of consumer demand. These pressures have had far-reaching implications for the clothing industry in the areas of pricing, design, quality, manufacturing processes and employment. It is not the intention here to discuss these changes in any great detail. Phizacklea (1990), Rainnie (1989) and Totterdill and Zeitlin (1989) have all provided thoroughgoing analyses of recent developments in the national and international clothing industry. Rather, the aim is to outline some of the important themes affecting the clothing industry nationally in order to set the scene for the more detailed study of the West Midlands clothing sector.

In the 1970s, the previously stable British market, with its well established characteristics of mass production, predictable design and long production runs, became increasingly vulnerable to newly industrialised countries like Hong Kong. Traditional British manufacturers, usually High Street retailers in the tradition of Burton's who had their own manufacturing capacity, found themselves unable to compete with low wage producers. Standard garments such as suits, rainwear and jeans, where year on year fashion changes tended to be minimal, were particularly susceptible to competition from low wage producers. Indeed some international manufacturers saw such developments as an opportunity to move their manufacturing operations to these newly industrialising, low wage countries. Up until 1976, the United Kingdom had been a net exporter of textile and clothing products. Despite the negotiation of quotas under the Multi-Fibre Arrangement (MFA), designed to stabilise market-production relationships, by the beginning of the 1980s imports were approaching 30% of the British clothing market (West Midlands Low Pay Unit [WMLPU], 1991)

The intensity of such competition had a dramatic effect on levels of employment; between the mid 1970s and the early 1980s, employment in garment manufacture fell by one third to less than 220,000. Such was the extent of the decline that it was thought clothing had become a 'sunset industry' (Davenport et al, 1986).

The 1980s, however, witnessed radical changes in the buying patterns of retailers which some argue provide an opportunity for British manufacturers to arrest the seemingly inexorable decline in their fortunes (Totterdill and Zeitlin, 1989). The preferences of U.K consumers has shifted, it is suggested, away from standardised mass produced garments to a less regimented, more unpredictable collection of individual items of clothing that reflect their 'lifestyle'. This is probably the result of some sophisticated marketing from prominent European companies. Perhaps the 'brand leader' in terms of this type of approach and the exemplar of new methods of garment manufacture is Benetton. Benetton effectively by-passed the domination of the previously ascendent British retailers by creating its own franchised network with direct links to its warehousing and manufacturing facilities in Italy (WMPLU, 1991).

Benetton's essential novelty lies in its information system which enables it to link up a network of wholesalers and retailers with large groups of producers. Through this information system, it is possible to rapidly identify the most successful styles, colours and designs. With manufacturing, dyeing and delivery systems geared to responding quickly to this sales information, the lead time between consumer preference and garment manufacture is extremely short. Moreover, the actual costs of manufacture are not borne by Benetton - all the labour intensive stages of production are sub-contracted out. Only the capital intensive processes are kept 'in-house'. Phizacklea (1990: 16) asserts that this strategy secures " the 'best of both worlds'; reaping the benefits of new technology and the cheaper costs of the sub-contracting system, while minimising risk and uncertainty."

Major British retailers have, to varying degrees, attempted to emulate the 'Benetton model'. The likes of the Burton Group, Sears, Storehouse and Next have concentrated on the retail sector and pursued a strategy of luring consumers away from relatively cheap mass marketed clothes to a new co-ordinated look combining high fashion with value for money (Phizacklea, 1990: 15). The emphasis appeared to have shifted to 'niche marketing' and 'customer differentiation'. Even the previously 'staid' Marks and Spencer seemed to have changed its marketing stance in an effort to demonstrate its receptiveness to the fluidity of fashion trends. The key elements were 'the move to a three fashion season with regular top-ups on orders throughout the season, the move towards much lower volume orders of higher quality goods and increasing reliance on design input from manufacturers' (Davenport, 1992: 6).

This 'retail revolution' had profound implications for the manufacturing of clothing. A concentration on fashion and quality necessitated a departure from garments produced in vast quantities and ordered twelve months or so before anticipated sale, to more consumer sensitive shorter runs and better designed products. Herein lay the opportunities for

British manufacturers. The complexities involved in relying on low cost producers in the Far East in terms of long delivery times, design and quality requirements lessened their attraction to retailers seeking quick response times and garments of a high standard. Manufacturing capacity, allied with production flexibility, needed to be much closer to the market. Retailers like Next, Principles and C and A attempted to pursue a more active policy of local sourcing; Next and Principles opted to purchase at least 75% of their clothing products from British suppliers. The most obvious advantage of local sourcing was that it avoided tying up large amounts of money in cloth, shipping and warehousing before it could be recovered from sales (WMPLU, 1991).

Whether or not British clothing manufacturers have grasped the opportunities generated by such developments in retail trends is a matter of debate (see Davenport, 1992). Firms may respond by investing in new technology, enhancing their design capability and competing in terms of quality and adaptability rather than price. Such a strategy could allow for better pay and conditions for clothing workers (Totterdill and Zeitlin, 1989). Alternatively, the changing nature of retailing could result in greater exploitation of homeworkers as firms become increasingly reliant on sub-contracting for flexibility and competitiveness (Mitter, 1985).

What is clear, however, is that the West Midlands clothing industry is immersed in a sector whose recent history is far from propitious and whose future is contingent upon the uncertainties of an increasingly competitive market (witness the arrival of the 'new' EC producers) and rapidly changing consumer preferences. The West Midlands clothing industry cannot hope to remain immune from such vicissitudes.

The West Midland Clothing Sector

Before the mid-1970s, clothing manufacture could not be regarded as a significant West Midlands industry. Employing around 7,000 workers, or less than 1% of the workforce in 1966, the industry then fell into decline during the following ten years. This decline was due primarily to the closure, for reasons of bankruptcy, of some of the large old-established firms in the men's outerwear and waterproof clothing sectors, which were the main areas of specialism within the West Midlands industry. The decline was accentuated by many large firms in the menswear sub-sector relocating from inner city areas to new factories in new towns and development areas (Hayden, 1992).

The first half of the 1970s witnessed a fall in the level of employment in the West Midlands clothing industry of 7.3% to less than 6,500. Since the mid-1970s however, there has been a marked increase in clothing sector employment due to the entry of new firms manufacturing untailored garments in the lower end of the market (Hayden, 1992). These predominantly Asian-owned companies have tended to develop flexible and relatively low cost production facilities. This in turn has led to a concentration on lower volume and untailored products such as work clothing and jeans, women's light outerwear and weatherproof outerwear. Within the last product area there seems to be a particular concentration on padded jackets, sports and leisure clothing and casual wear, rather than on tailored raincoats and overcoats. These products typically involve short run lengths and relatively simple production methods (Mawson, 1988).

The area of general untailored outerwear is thought to account for about 500 mainly small firms in the West Midlands area (although the situation is unclear given the existence of many unregistered workshops and the prevalence of homeworking). The main concentrations (in decreasing order of importance) are in inner Birmingham, Smethwick, Coventry, Wolverhampton, West Bromwich and Walsall. In comparison, there is a maximum of 50 older firms throughout the region producing tailored garments and more formal outerwear. The total number of workers now employed in the West Midlands clothing industry is difficult to establish with precision given the prevalence of 'informal' working practices, but it is estimated to be between 20,000 and 30,000 workers (WMLPU, 1991).

The rapid rise of clothing sector employment in the West Midlands during the 1980s, which was in excess of 20%, was in marked contrast to the position nationally. In 1981, employment in the U.K clothing industry was 221,000, by 1987 it had fallen to 206,000 and by the end of 1989 it had declined further to 200,000 - a decrease of 9.5%. Why did the West Midlands buck the national trend? The next section discusses why Asians turned to the clothing industry in such numbers.

Getting Started

Scase and Goffee (1987: 11-19) speculate on a number of reasons why people start their own business. Some might see it as an opportunity to make a lot of money in a short period - they might want to become entrepreneurial 'heroes', possibly millionaires. Others turn to self-employment in an attempt to overcome the disadvantage that they face in the labour market: 'historically, entrepreneurship has enabled members of ethnic, religious and other minority groups to achieve personal success'(p14). Then there are those who set up on their own so that they can gain greater control over their lives and not have to be accountable to anyone else for their actions. Finally, self-employment or setting up a small business might be the only way that individuals can use their talents to the full, talent which may be under-utilised in their present occupations.

There are, then, a variety of reasons why people start their own business; but after asking in excess of one hundred small employers the question, 'why start your own business ?', Scase and Goffee came to the conclusion that " Business formation and growth is often not the outcome of exceptional personal capacities of drive, determination and ambition, but a function of various forms of personal discontent ... setting up a business ... was a conscious decision to 'drop-out' " (p33). People 'dropped-out' in the sense that they rejected employee status or sought an alternative life-style not based on an imperative of being accountable to someone else.

On the basis of this evidence, self-employment is the product of choice, although the 'rationality' of that choice may be open to question. It is doubtful, however, whether ethnic minorities have the same degree of choice. The debate on minority enterprise reviewed earlier noted that despite the variety of explanations accounting for the growth of ethnic business, the high incidence of ethnic enterprise was more a response to the lack of opportunity elsewhere than the internal characteristics of the minority group.

This was borne out by the respondents in the current study. The responses to the question 'Why did you start your own business' were all quite similar. Most employers expressed the view that to become self-employed was the only route to advancement and earning a decent living. It was a choice between menial factory work or setting up in business and, therefore, perhaps the chance of something better. They did not possess any significant expertise or flair for clothing. None had received training in any formal sense and few had any real experience of management or running a business. They tended to be former machinists or factory workers who turned to clothing because it was cheap, the purchase of a few machines being sufficient to get the venture off the ground.

It was not only the unskilled, however, who turned to self-employment as a means of advancement. Even highly trained Asians found themselves looking to the clothing industry because of the paucity of opportunity in mainstream employment. One such Asian was a graduate in electronic engineering. He sought a career in this area but found it extremely difficult securing employment. When he did find work it was usually low level, low paid and not commensurate with his level of training. Another employer, who was a master's level graduate, also found himself turning to clothing because of the dearth of opportunity elsewhere. After graduating in 1981, he decided against a career because " There seemed to be very few opportunities for black graduates. The clothing industry was the only one that I knew since my friends were involved in it, so I got into it".

For many Asians, in addition to the prospect of menial work, the threat of unemployment and redundancy was also very real, and so acted as a further spur to self-employment. Many companies were started during the periods of economic austerity in the 1970s and the 1980s. This turns the notion of 'enterprise culture' on its head. The rise of the ethnic business sector was more a product of racism and recession than of the government's encouragement of small business.

An appreciation of this context is, then, crucial to understanding why so many ethnic minority men are located in this particular sector of the clothing industry. It was not so much that they 'dropped-out', as Scase and Goffee conclude in the case of their small employers; minority men were forced out - forced out of mainstream employment and forced into self-employment. Entrepreneurship, for many, represented the only route out of the dole and the drudgery of factory work. The promise of rich pickings was often illusory. Of the sixteen proprietors interviewed, seven revealed their wages and in no case did it exceed £150 per week. Some claimed that they only took money for general expenses, preferring to leave the rest in the business. It was clear that some of these owners were struggling, as one claimed , " We're just working to survive ". It seems, as Phizacklea (1990: 5) puts it " "Their position is rarely that of a rags to Mercedes immigrant, but more of a transition from the lumpenproletatriat to becoming a member of the lumpenbourgeosie. "

Most such entrepreneurs are concentrated in the 'dog eat dog' end of the market where margins are tight, competition is intense and new technology is largely absent. All the respondents in the survey stage of the study claimed that the market that they were in had become increasingly competitive over the last three years or so, and expected it to become even greater in the future. The actual composition of the market needs to be examined more closely since an appreciation of the pressures that it generates is important in accounting for the nature of management in the West Midlands clothing industry. It is not simply a question of powerful retailers dominating individual garment manufacturers. Clothing firms in the West Midlands are enmeshed in a rather more complex, informal and unpredictable market. Although the competitive pressures of operating in such a market are no less intense than those identified by Rainnie in his more general study, the market is, nevertheless, different and needs to be explored in greater detail.

Marketing Relationships

General surveys of local clothing companies in 1984 (Handsworth Technical College) and 1988 (Lewis) revealed that over 90% of sales went through intermediaries. Only two companies in this study supplied chainstores directly, and it was noticeable that these firms were quite satisfied with their relationship with the stores and expressed most optimism about the future. However, this was at a price, as was exemplified by one chainstore supplier. The owner revealed that he had to disclose to the retailer the source of the fabric used, the supplier, its composition and price. The retailer required this information to protect supplies in the event of the manufacturer going out of business and needing to switch production if an increase in capacity was required. The proprietor also had to reveal the cost of the garment and the mark-up.

Those manufacturers supplying chainstores through agents (four) voiced a certain ambivalence over their relationship with these intermediaries. They received fairly regular orders from the agents which they appeared grateful for. However, there was also a feeling that they were being used by the agent (who was the same in all four cases). The owners believed that different companies were being paid different rates for the same product. The greater the capacity and the greater the negotiating ability of the individual owner, the greater the eventual rate was likely to be. These companies were being used to 'top-up' orders. The chainstores tend to place the bulk of their orders in countries like Portugal. It was, however, difficult to re-order from foreign concerns because their turn-around period was three months as opposed to two weeks in these four companies. Furthermore, it was acknowledged by the owners that their main point of competitiveness was price and unless this was reflected in their dealings with the agents, they would lose the business.

Given these concerns about the role of agents, why did these companies remain with them? Two mutually reinforcing reasons were articulated. Firstly, they felt that they lacked the necessary marketing skills to deal direct with buyers from chainstores. Secondly, there was a feeling that chainstores would not deal directly with companies like theirs. It was felt that Asian firms were perceived as unreliable, low standard and exploitative. Hence using white agents with access to buyers from large chainstores was a necessary strategy in the quest for regular orders.

Wholesalers were the most popular market for manufacturers. Seven firms in the sample supplied wholesalers, and in most cases, their entire production went to such outlets. These wholesalers were also Asian-owned concerns. Most manufacturers felt that wholesalers showed little loyalty to them, and that the situation was exacerbated by competition from other manufacturers who realised that this was the easiest market to get into. Wholesalers were regarded as fickle and often played one manufacturer off against another.

Four of the companies were Cut Make and Trim (CMT) operations. It was apparent that these firms were being used by larger manufacturers to meet periods of intense demand. When this period elapses, their services are discarded. However, there is no simple cut-off point. Often the larger companies attempt to keep the smaller concerns dependent on them even in the quieter period by asking them to make for stock, with the expectation that the stock will be purchased at a later date when demand picks up. Sometimes, this stock remains with the CMT firm and they have to dispose of it, often at a loss. Furthermore, the irregular nature of orders, and the fact that the orders tend to be small and involve almost continual style changes, poses problems in production since such changes puts pressure on machinists.

This market situation seems to lend credence to an observation arising from a recent survey,

" The typical West Midlands untailored outwear company ... finds itself within a complex web of relationships between suppliers, other producers and retailers. In addition, most of these will be much larger than the individual company and with substantial market power. Given that the end product itself is increasingly subject to fashion changes and demanding requirements concerning price, style and quality, the company is constantly subject to a wide range of intense competitive pressures " (Mawson, 1988: 6).

The nature of these trading relationships reveals two important points. Management within small clothing companies, as in many small firms, often lacks the necessary skills to break out of the bottom end of the market and grasp opportunities that the wider market may hold. Secondly, the activities of customers, be they retailers or larger manufacturers, impose significant constraints on the development of small clothing companies.

The dearth of trained and skilled managers served to perpetuate the precarious position of the firm in the market. Despite the potentially greater rewards of moving 'up-market' manufacturers appeared to be locked into the lower end of the market. None of the managers interviewed were trained in any formal sense, a feature which was not surprising given their reasons for entering the trade discussed earlier. An earlier survey identified management training as 'the biggest need and ... an essential pre-requisite to all other company development' (Lewis, 1988). One can see the effect of this lack of expertise in typical clothing firms in the West Midlands. Good garment design and innovation, for instance, is crucial if decent margins are to be secured, but rarely is it evident in such concerns.

At the design stage, a designer creates a design that is subsequently made into a rough pattern. However, designers in this sector are rare. Only two firms out of the sixteen visited employed or used the services of a designer, and they tended to be the more 'up-market' firms supplying chainstores directly. If these companies wanted to keep the custom of the chainstores, then they had to come up with new designs continually, a point that was forcibly made by Gel, the de facto managing director of company C, "Sometimes you make samples and samples and nothing will come of them. A hell of a lot of sample making is involved if you're going to get any orders. " The production of sample garments was very time consuming and expensive, yet they had to be supplied to all potential customers if orders were to be secured.

The Cut, Make and Trim firms, by definition, had no design function. They simply assembled garments from work provided for them by larger manufacturers. Although for firms fortunate enough to be receiving regular orders this provided a modicum of stability, the problem was that margins were extremely narrow, as one proprietor said in resignation, 'We don't make any money'.

For manufacturers supplying wholesalers, the design function seemed to entail merely producing the cheapest copy of an established garment or modifying a sample garment provided by the customer. There was little if any investment in producing original designs or anticipating future trends. In the months of January and February, and July and August, manufacturers are often at their most frantic desperately seeking a 'line' that will see them through the summer and winter respectively. During these months, it is not uncommon to find local manufacturers roaming the retail outlets of stores like Marks and Spencer and C and A. What tends to happen is that these manufacturers will purchase garments from these stores which they believe that they may be able to produce and sell. They make a rough pattern from the garment, and then duly return the garment to the store and collect a refund. This constituted the design function for two companies that I have worked for.

The second feature of the trading relationships of typical clothing companies in the West Midlands identified was the activities of customers, which served to constrain the smaller firms. To this one could add the practices of the larger fabric suppliers. Once a design has been accepted by the customer, manufacturers need to ensure that they have adequate supplies of fabric with which to produce the garment. Material commonly accounts for approximately half the total cost of the finished garment, and material quality is obviously an important selling point when negotiating with customers. Many West Midlands firms have to rely on local cloth merchants who are willing to supply relatively small amounts of material and extend credit. The range of cloth is often quite narrow and not the kind that the 'quality' stores would necessarily be interested in.

The restricted choice is due to the fact British producers of textiles are geared primarily towards servicing high volume garment manufacturers. Firms wishing to move into higher quality product areas in order to get a higher proportion of their business from major retailers are often unable to do so because they do not receive the required level of service from fabric suppliers. These fabric suppliers impose minimum order requirements that are too high, they have excessive lead times (because they give preference to the larger manufacturers) and insist on harsh credit terms. Manufacturers therefore have to arrange their own direct imports or place orders with wholesalers, both options involving extra costs (Mawson, 1988).

Given the constellation of these pressures, an obvious consequence of this type of market situation is uncertainty. Intense competition, fickle customers, tight delivery times, rapid changes in fashion and the seasonal nature of the industry served to create a high level of uncertainty amongst manufacturers. When asked what their expectations were in relation to output over the next three years, the responses were necessarily vague. Few employers could give answers informed by orders already secured. Although most anticipated an increase in production in the coming years, this was a view based on hope rather than expectation. Manufacturers rarely had advance orders of more than a few months. One manufacturer who was totally reliant on wholesalers stated that he was not in a position of knowing what to do from one week to the next.

An Insight into Uncertainty

Discussions with Gel, the de facto managing director of company C, revealed the bewildering nature of the uncertainties facing such employers. Gel claimed that in order to make an average garment, approximately fifteen operations or tasks would have to be performed. The right material had to be sourced and available in sufficient quantity. It has to be marked and cut with precision. It is also necessary to ensure that the appropriate number and quality of zips, thread and other accessories that may be needed for the garment can be supplied. At that point in time, a particular order, which had an agreed delivery date, had to be delayed for two weeks because Gel had just found out that the required fabric would not be arriving as scheduled. The company had to let another order go because they 'couldn't get the material'.

After the problem with material came the 'headache of labour' as Gel described it. The nature of shopfloor organisation and supervision will be considered in more detail in subsequent chapters, but it is apposite here to mention briefly how this employer felt that labour contributed towards uncertainty. Each garment is assembled by machinists who are responsible for sewing a particular part of the garment rather than the garment as a whole. A typical group of machinists will include workers responsible for linings, joining, pockets and finishing. Furthermore, the different operations are sequential so, for example, the pockets of the garment cannot be attached before the linings are completed. Consequently, not only must the machinists be continually supplied with work so they are kept 'busy', the right proportion of the right work must be allocated to the right machinist if imbalances in the production flow are to be avoided.

However, even if the flow of work is smooth, the most meticulous planning can be disrupted by the activities of the machinists. If particular machinists are absent, and Gel claims that three or four are 'away all the time', then the whole sequence can be thrown out of balance. Other machinists might have to be given different work in order to compensate for the absences. It was not unusual for the delivery date to be extended because of the erratic attendance of the machinists. The 'unreliability' of the machinists was cited by Gel as the company's biggest problem, "They come and go as they please and work in their own way. But you can't punish them, they'll leave and go somewhere else and punish you."

In addition to the pressures of production and rapid changes of fashion, customers will often impose tight deadlines and even tighter margins, " You're spending £8 in order to make £2." During the busy period, 'you're grabbing orders from everywhere and just praying that you can make them'. Retailers were using Gel's company to 'top-up' their supply'. Gel claimed that, 'They [the retailers] don't want us to make the bulk orders, they'll get them made from the Far East, Portugal or Spain. They'll say that they need the order in two weeks or they'll take the business elsewhere'.

Even when the goods have been distributed, there is an anxious wait before payment is received, " They [the customers] will use any little excuse to delay paying you. It just takes one bad debt to wipe out your profit for the whole order. " Customers might, for example, claim that the garment has not quite matched specifications and duly demand a reduction in price or threaten to return the goods altogether.

Little wonder that Gel says, " If I had a choice, I'd get out of it. I've got too many headaches. I worry about whether or not I can pay this or that person, if I've got the design right, if we can get the production. It gets to the stage where you can't sleep at night."

This insight into the uncertainties of the environment that employers like Gel have to operate in offers a clear illustration of Hyman's point concerning the difficulty of harmonising the different functions of management. The extent of uncertainty produced contradictory pressures. There was a need to keep costs down, the main component of which is labour in a labour intensive industry. However, there was also a need to maintain sufficient capacity to respond quickly to surges in demand and accommodate rapid style changes. How was this uncertainty managed on a more general level?

Given the structure of the industry, one might expect that the immense pressures that West Midland clothing manufacturers are subjected to would create a situation whereby authoritarian management would be necessary if they are to survive. There seems to be a fairly widespread view that the viability of the sector rests upon the intensive use of Asian female labour working either from home or in small sweatshops (Leigh and North, 1983: Mitter, 1985: Phizacklea, 1987). Phizacklea, for example, claims that "The prime means of maintaining profitability amongst small, secondary sector firms, is the extraction of surplus value through intensification and casualisation of work " (1990: 20). Mitter has outlined the stark exploitation of homeworkers generally while Hoel's (1982) study of Asian women workers in a Coventry clothing company highlights the autocratic nature of management in such concerns and suggests that certain cultural customs reinforced management's power over the machinists.

The actual workplace evidence for claims of this kind, however, appears to be limited. What constitutes the 'intensive use of labour' in this context has not really been explored, yet it is presented as integral to the survival of many clothing manufacturers in the sector. There is little doubt that low wages, long hours and dubious employment practices, such as the evasion of national insurance contributions, are widespread. Indeed some of the survey findings from the current research support such claims. It is a lowly paid industry with the average wage for a machinist being around £80 (This, however, was the 'official' rate. Many employers claimed that the real rate was significantly higher), machinists work long hours and the actual working environment of many such establishments is not particularly congenial. However, the casualisation and intensification of labour is not necessarily as simple, nor as 'rational', as the survey evidence and general statements indicate. The next section critically examines these points.

Casualisation

The use of external labour, that is, homeworkers and sub-contractors, is certainly an important mechanism used by employers to come to terms with the vagaries of the market. Not surprisingly, precise figures on the number of homeworkers are difficult to obtain, but an earlier survey (Handsworth Technical College, 1984) estimated that for every on-site worker, there were two homeworkers. A notable feature was the comparatively small number of homeworkers used by firms on the one hand (52) and the apparently widespread use of sub-contractors on the other (27 units were used by the 12 firms hiring sub-contractors). One possible explanation for this is the expense and general inconvenience that employers incur when dealing with individual homeworkers. Employers have to cut, bundle, batch and deliver the various components of garments to individual homeworkers and then collect the finished product. Owners may therefore find it easier to deal with a broker, who will have his or her network of homeworkers and will undertake these tasks, for a fee.

The companies deploying homeworkers, did, nevertheless, use them regularly and there was no real difference between the work that they did and the work of the on-site workers. Not all these outworkers were, however, classified as employees by the owners, yet there were no definite criteria used by them to determine why one homeworker should be treated as an employee and not another. It appeared that the decision to grant employee status to homeworkers was an informal, particularistic and variable one.

Employers regarded the use of homeworkers and sub-contractors as the only way production could be increased and as a mechanism for flexibility. This was exemplified by the fact that, in all cases, homeworkers and sub-contractors were, apparently, the first to go when there was a slow down in demand.

But, in dealings with homeworkers and sub-contractors, the relationship was not simply a 'hire and fire' one. As mentioned earlier, larger manufacturers endeavoured to keep smaller firms dependent on them even during the quiet season by encouraging them to make for stock. In relation to homeworkers, employers tried to maintain this dependent relationship by supplying work in a 'drip, drip' fashion.

As I accompanied Sig, a partner in company B, to the home of an outworker on a January day, he remarked "When work is slack you avoid them like the plague." Homeworkers had been trying to contact Sig for days in an effort to find out when they could expect more work. They had actually been given work but only in dribs and drabs. Since it was the quiet season, they were unlikely to receive work from other quarters. Furthermore, despite the fact that they were employees, they were also on piecerate and, accordingly, received no compensatory payments. A similar situation prevailed in company A. This was the comment of a homeworker to whom I had just delivered some work, " They starve us of work then only deliver parts of the garment, making it impossible for us to complete it without nagging for the rest of the stuff." Although the homeworker was an experienced machinist, he had not produced this particular garment before, yet he had been sent various parts of the garment in random order to be getting on with. He had not been given a sample of the garment in question nor any clear instructions.

When the 'busy' season arrives, however, sub-contractors and homeworkers can find themselves in a position where they can negotiate more effectively for better rates and choose which orders to take. Their position, as a consequence, is not static; they do have a 'seasonal' power. For example, it was the middle of the busy season and Sig from company B had noted that some of the sub-contractors that he had used were putting up their prices. Sig claimed that this was a common practice at this time of the year,

> " They [the sub-contractors] have gone through the bad patch and can now see some light at the end of the tunnel, so they're asking thirty or forty pence more for a garment. This one sub-contractor is demanding stupid prices. A jacket that he made for £8.40 during the quiet period, he won't make for £9 now. But, come the quiet period again, he'll drop his price. Everything depends on whose got the upper hand, and that depends on the season."

In turn, however, Sig claimed that the company could be more selective about its own customers. At the present time, the firm could 'pick and choose'. A major customer of company B (which was effectively a Cut, Make and Trim business) sent a sample that they wanted the firm to produce. The management examined it and believed that they could make it. However, they were very busy at the time, " We're not really that bothered." But the customer was applying pressure. Sig responded by quoting an 'inflated price', £15.30 for a jacket that they would, in other circumstances, be prepared to make for £13. An eventual price of £15 (for an order of 1100 garments, which is considered an average run) was negotiated with an extended delivery date.

Company A relied heavily on external labour and so tried hard to keep favoured sub-contractors supplied with work even though the orders were not always there. In the summer of 1988, the company failed to produce a viable 'summer' jacket. Given that the company's main outlet was the wholesale market, where lead times were around ten days, this meant that the firm was receiving very little income between February and August of that year. However, it could not risk letting its main sub-contractors go since they would be needed when demand eventually picked up. The proprietor decided to keep the sub-contractors supplied with 'winter' jackets throughout the summer despite the fact that he did not have any concrete orders for the garments.

The use of external labour therefore was an important means of coming to terms with the uncertainties and vagaries of the particular market that these manufacturers were in. However, as the case study evidence shows, the relationship between manufacturers and external labour was not simply a 'hire and fire' one, as it often tends to be portrayed. Homeworkers and sub-contractors undoubtedly afforded manufacturers a certain flexibility which was crucial to a quick response to market fluctuations. The use of such labour, rather than investment in new technology or more 'efficient' working methods, was seen by management as the only way that they could increase production quickly, as they were required to do if they were to meet the increasingly short lead times demanded by the customer.

However, in many cases, manufacturers could not simply jettison the external labour when there was a fall off in demand. To do so might render employers incapable of delivering the goods when demand picked up. Hence manufacturers often used tactics like the 'drip drip' approach described earlier or they just kept them supplied with garments that they hoped would sell at a later date. These decisions were risk laden, complex and not entirely consistent with the received image of authoritarian management.

Allied to the process of casualisation, the general perception seems to be that the sector survives through the intensive use of labour, particularly ethnic and familial labour. The actual detail of shopfloor organisation will be developed more fully in the chapter four. The next section is concerned with how management seeks to organise production at the level of the workplace and copes with the uncertainties occasioned by the market. Key to these issues is the role of the family in the management of the firm.

Family Labour

The Family in Management

The intensive use of familial labour is widely seen as an important factor in explaining the viability of minority enterprise (Mars and Ward,1984). Family members are expected to work 'hard'. They are expected to have the interests of the firm at heart and to do whatever is necessary to ensure the survival and prosperity of the firm,

> "When we're busy, we [the family] work all hours " claimed Parg of company C. According to Sig, a partner in company B, " The burden is shared - finance, trust, risk - it's all shared. I'm not the owner of the factory, but I worry if production is not coming out or if the accounts are not in order. If one of us have to go somewhere, then we know that there's someone left in the factory that we can trust. You can rely on family members to do the work, you can't really do that with ordinary workers."

I accompanied Sig on a visit to his solicitor. On our return, he made the following point in relation to family and 'trust',

> " Look, we've just been to the solicitor's. I had to wait in a queue and on my way back, I popped home for a few minutes. No questions were asked when I got back because they (the other family members) know that I have the company's interests at heart. If it had been an ordinary worker, it would be different. He'd be put on the spot and asked why he took so long."

Seemingly irrespective of their position in the firm, family members were expected to monitor what was going on. When I was in company A one day, I was asked to 'keep an eye on Fee'. Fee was one of the company's most senior and 'trusted' employees. In a company that I was familiar with in the survey stage of the study, Gill, who was a senior supervisor, claimed that the proprietor used his sister, a machinist, to 'spy' on her and everyone else on the shopfloor, " Information was getting to Sham [the proprietor] that I certainly did not provide."

The companies in the survey stage of the study were all family-owned concerns with members of the family occupying the key management and supervisory positions within the firms. Typically, the company would be managed by the men in the family and the machinists would be supervised by the women in the family, who were often the spouses of the managers. The position of the family in the three case study firms will now be looked at in more detail.

In company C these were the positions of the family in the firm,

Par	-	General management
Gel	-	De facto managing director, design and pattern-making
Sat	-	Lay-marking and cutting
Bugs	-	Lay-marking and cutting
Harj	-	Sales
Dev	-	Quality control (packing!)
Prem	-	Quality control
Perm (Prem's wife)	-	Supervision
Suneta (Gel's wife)	-	Sample machinist
Rani (Sat's wife)	-	Machinist

On the shopfloor where the machinists were situated, there were three family members, two of whom (Suneta and Perm) occupied important managerial roles. Perm was the senior supervisor, and it was her job to monitor the quality of the garments and to ensure that the machinists were kept supplied with work. If management wanted to communicate any specific instructions to the machinists, they would convey the message through her. According to Perm, " The men look after the men, the women look after the women." If orders had to be completed urgently, it would be Perm who would 'chivvy' the machinists along. Alternatively, if the machinists had any particular grievance, over the rate or faulty cutting for example, they would go to Perm and she, in turn, would communicate with management.

Suneta was given the job of sample machinist because, according Gel, they needed someone that they could 'trust' to tell them how difficult a particular garment was to assemble and what would be a fair rate for the job. Her views on the complexities of garments were integral to the calculation of the piece-rate.

In the cutting area, the quite complex tasks of lay-planning, marking and cutting were all undertaken by male members of the family. These were key positions within the firm. In order to understand fully the division of labour in the cutting area, it is important to have an appreciation of the nature of the tasks that are performed at this particular stage of production. Lay-planning involves laying out and arranging the various elements of the garment pattern so as to ensure optimum fabric utilisation. This process usually involves the creation of a paper marker. The various elements of the pattern are laid out and arranged on the cloth indicating the optimum lay of the pattern on the cloth.

Since the material comprises half of the cost of the garment, this is a crucial stage. Making minor adjustments here and there can save money. Consequently, this task is usually performed by a family member. This was a comment of a family member in company C who was responsible for marking and cutting garments,

" Space is very important in this game [in order to ensure maximum fabric utilisation]. You need someone you can trust to do this, that's why only the family are allowed to do it. Other people don't care, they'll just mark it any old way, not in the best way. If you can save five inches on a lay of around a thousand garments, then you can save up to seven hundred pounds. It's enough for a holiday."

For the proprietor of company A, 'expediency' at this stage was common practice. One ploy was to use imperfect material, that is, 'seconds', wherever possible. If the patterns were suitably arranged around the flaws then it was often possible to 'get away with it'. Another trick was to use inferior material in the linings of the sleeves. It seems that very few customers check sleeve linings when they purchase garments.

At the next stage, the cloth is spread on to a large table from a roller. In large firms, this is usually done by an automatic spreading machine. In most local companies, however, the cloth is spread manually, a process that involves two people walking in parallel alongside the table unfurling the cloth as they go along. The paper marker is placed on top of the layers and the lay is then ready to be cut. The cutting equipment is usually a hand held power driven reciprocating blade. Once the cutting is complete, the cut pieces are tied into bundles and then distributed to the machinists.

In company B, the tasks of lay-planning, marking and cutting were again performed by family members and they too sought ways to become more 'efficient' in this area. They receive a computerised lay-plan from their customers from which they are supposed to work to. However, Sig claimed that 'The computer is inefficient'. He will mark the lay again trimming and manipulating the shapes here and there. This makes no difference to the appearance of the final product yet often leads to a 10% reduction in the amount of material used.

Most of the time of family members in company B was spent on these and related activities. There seemed to be very little time devoted to management in any strategic sense. In the machinists' room, however, there were no family members. Instead management relied on what Sig called 'trustees'. Sig claimed that there were certain women whom 'you can trust to give you a fair opinion of a price of a garment'. These machinists, according to Sig, had 'proved themselves over the years by being honest and reliable. You give them work to do without agreeing a price and they come back with a price that is similar or less than yours'.

Within company A, other than Phu, there were no family members involved in the day-to-day running of the business, although the sons, Sol, Bas and myself, did assist to varying degrees. This meant that key activities that would normally be performed by members of the family were now in the hands of two particular workers, Fee (sales) and Gee (cutting).

Both Fee and Gee, who claimed that they enjoyed the trust of the proprietor, had considerable discretion over their work and felt a personal responsibility and obligation towards their employer. Fee has worked in the business in varying capacities for over ten years and cites the 'respect' that he has been treated with as a major reason for him being there so long,

> " I want to work hard and repay that respect. When I go on a delivery or go to collect money from customers, I look upon it as though I am doing the job for myself. I'm not an ordinary worker who will always be watching the time, I'll do what is required."

This sense of loyalty was reinforced by parental pressure. On occasions when Fee had been in dispute with the proprietor, Fee's parents were called in to help reach a settlement. Gee also appeared to exemplify this attitude. He was responsible for the quite complex tasks of marking and cutting garments as well as negotiating with customers. He recognised that he had an important role in the company, but also realised that he was allowed this degree of freedom and responsibility because there is no member of the proprietor's family who was in a position to take his job.

Gee readily admitted that he was not working there solely for the money. The degree of discretion that he was allowed is crucial to explaining his longevity at the firm. He is aware that it would be unlikely that he could assume a such a role in another clothing firm, since in most similar concerns members of the family perform such functions. He is well aware that he is heavily relied upon and that the consequences of him adopting an 'ordinary worker's' attitude to the job would be significant. Nevertheless. He sometimes did,

" When I'm pissed off, I'll go home at lunch time and not come back or sometimes I'll just take the day off."

" What is the proprietor's reaction ? " (M.R)

" Well, he doesn't lecture me. He just asks me if the reason for my absence was important. All that I have to say is 'yes' and the matter is left."

This was borne out by Phu's reaction, or rather, non-reaction , to Gee's absence when I was on the premises, " The fucking bastard still hasn't turned up. He spent half the day yesterday messing about and he's still not here yet. Today's going to be wasted. He's supposed to be getting a sample ready for the machinists to sew, but he's still not here. The day's wasted." Gee did not come in that day.

The following day, I asked Gee why he did not turn up. He said that he had to go to London. When I asked why he did not let anyone know, he replied that he did not have to and that he would take time off when he wanted to. He was not reprimanded by Phu despite the fact that his absence caused difficulties.

In attempting to explain why such workers were allowed this degree of autonomy, it is important to appreciate that there was a major element of reciprocity in such arrangements. Gee realised that if he took a day off, he would be expected to make it up at a later date. The proprietor, Phu, put up with the bad time-keeping and the absences because there was no one to replace him. Hence, an informal bargain seemed to have been struck. Gee could have his 'unofficial flexi-time' as long as the time was made up later. He could have the reward of enjoyable duties, like dealing with customers, as long as the machinists were kept supplied with work.

In Fee's case, the obligation that he felt towards the company stemmed from the 'favours and help' that the proprietor had afforded to him in the past. For example, the proprietor had extended a loan to Fee so that he could finance his wedding. Such favours serve to create a dependency on the employer and tie the worker more closely to the firm. It was a means of securing trust and consent and, to a certain extent, obviated the need forclose supervision. This did not necessarily mean that such workers would not engage in activities that management disapproved of. Fee's 'long' delivery times and Gee's erratic attendance were a continual source of tension. However, they seemed to recognise that certain tasks had to be done and accepted personal responsibility for them.

The social relations between Phu and 'key' workers like Gee and Fee were not the product of deliberate or planned strategy. They were the contradictory outcomes of an 'agency' relationship, which Armstrong contends is a 'core feature of management within capitalist social relations' (1989: 307). This relationship contains contradictions between the dependence of employers and managers on trust, and the fact that it is expensive, which gives them (employers) an incentive to dispense with it in favour of deskilling and the monitoring of managerial work. In companies B and C, the potential for conflict in this area was minimised by the placing of family members in key positions within the firm. The proprietor of company A did not have the option of replacing such key workers with family members. An attempt was made, however, six years ago to do precisely this. A son (myself) was being trained as a cutter/lay planner with the intention that he would replace Gee once he achieved sufficient competency. This policy was unsuccessful because the son left the firm and, as a consequence, the ambivalent relationship between Phu and Gee continues.

Familial Labour - A Constraint

The intensive use of familial labour then was an important means of managing the enterprise in this context. Where it was absent, as in the case of company A, the social relations were markedly different and much more unpredictable. Extensive familial involvement is depicted as a boon to management, primarily because it is cheap and supervision is made easier. Viewed in this way, the 'rationality' of the use of family labour seems beyond contention. However, the use of the family in key positions can, in important respects, serve to constrain management.

Some of the brothers in company C were not competent to hold the positions that they occupied but they were retained regardless. This was the comment of the only non-brother in a management role,

> " They're bosses but not all of them have the skill. Take Dev [a brother] for example. They spent £20,000 on a machine for him to run yet it's not making any money. They can't tell him to bugger off because he's a member of the family, but if it was me who was not pulling his weight, they'd soon tell me to piss off."

Pia, a cutting assistant and non-family worker, asserted that " The family attachments are preventing the firm from progressing. You need skilled people to organise. What you get is people organising because they're related to the boss rather than having any real expertise."

The brother with overall responsibility in company C stated that one of the problems of having so many members of the family in the business is that they 'take too many liberties'. On one occasion, the youngest brother, who was regarded as something of a 'playboy', was actually sacked. He was soon reinstated however because the parents applied pressure on the brother in charge. Clearly, 'controlling' a family member was not a simple process as the following exchange on the cutting room floor of company C illustrated,

Sat (to me) "No-one here tells me what to do, I just know what to do and I do it."
Gel (managing director) "I need three linings now."
Sat "Do them yourself, I've got better things to do."
There was no response from Gel.
Sat continued to me, "In Indian family firms, there's no bosses. I mean, if you tell him off (pointing to Bugs, another brother), he probably won't come back tomorrow."
"So you can't sack him ?" (M.R)
Sat "No, you can't do that. They can go if they want, it's up to them, but you can't sack them."

The 'problem' of eliciting of greater 'responsibility' from family members actually occasioned a change in the company structure. During the course of the fieldwork, the brothers in company C decided to split the firms into five divisions: Co. C, Trimmings, Wholesale, Laminating and Style Co. Each unit was to be treated as a profit centre with their own accounts and administration. According to the only non-family member in management,

" Before, there were too many gaffers and not enough workers. All the brothers wanted to sit behind the big desk in the office. They'd be wandering round doing very little and taking long tea and lunch breaks. No one was taking any responsibility. Now, the brothers have their own company to run, they have their own responsibility."

This view was echoed by Gel. He claimed that the move was designed to instil greater responsibility in the brothers, some of whom, he asserted, were 'riding on the backs' of others. The company was split not because of any commercial criteria,

"The company was split not because there was any demand from the market for such a move, it was just to give them [the brothers] something to do. Now they have a responsibility to make it profitable. At the end of they year, we can look at the accounts and performance of each company. If one isn't making any money, we can ask why. They know now that if they don't work, they won't get paid. Before, everyone used to get paid regardless of what they did. Now they have to earn money from their own companies. Each company will have to pay its own way" (Gel). Despite this assertion, there was an admission that brothers who failed to perform would be 'baled out'.

In spite of this attempt to secure greater responsibility, Gel conceded that 'efficiency' and the family were not really compatible, "Really, to run this place, you don't need more than two people, but we have the rest here because they're family." Gel could personally be in a better financial position if he were to branch out on his own. He often talked about his desire to set up his own company specialising in direct selling at the cutting edge of the fashion trade. However, he remained with the firm because he felt an 'obligation' to the family.

In company A, the relationship between the proprietor, Phu, and Gee exemplified the way in which the ascendency of the family sometimes led to management acting less than rationally. Explaining why he worked so hard, Gee said,

" I have to, people rely on me. For example, I didn't really want to come in on Bank Holiday Monday, but Phu forced me to. You see, this order was due on Thursday. If it was to be ready by then, I had to get the work cut on the Monday so that the machinists could have it on Tuesday morning."

The word 'force' was not used in a coercive sense. In this particular situation, Phu impressed upon Gee the need to have the order out by Thursday. Had Gee refused, it would have been unlikely that Phu would have imposed any kind of sanction. An appeal was made to his special position within the organisation, "I respond to the responsibility that I am given " claimed Gee.

The extent of this responsibility is, however, inexplicit, informal, vague and a source of tension. Clearly Gee is Phu's right hand man. He was certainly more aware of what was going on than Phu, especially on matters relating to garment construction and the distribution of work. If the concern was solely to increase the effective use of time, then Gee should undoubtedly have spent more of his time on lay-planning, monitoring quality and ensuring that the flow of work to the machinists was regular and co-ordinated. The skill element of these functions was significantly higher than cutting, the physical laying of material and tying the bundles of cut work. Yet Gee spent a considerable proportion of his time on these comparatively less demanding tasks. Gee was aware of this and would have liked to have spent a greater proportion of time on the more skilled tasks. Why had this not occurred ? Gee's response to this question was " Phu ".To have formalised Gee's role in this way would have meant that he had even more latitude. The monitoring of quality, for example, would have required Gee to spend much of his time off the premises since most of the output comes from sub-contractors. Phu would see this as an erosion of his power. The purchase of material from local suppliers, in which Gee was sporadically involved, would have been an area where he could have been more directly employed. His knowledge of shading, density and general appropriateness of cloth would have been very useful. However, since the overwhelming majority of suppliers were of the Asian community, to have Gee in such an influential position could be taken as a signal that perhaps the family was not in complete control of the firm. Phu would be extremely reluctant to cede so much power to someone who was not a member of his family, or more specifically, a son.

The evidence drawn from these case studies demonstrates that although casualisation and the use of familial labour in management were widespread and seemingly 'rational', they were policies that were not entirely efficacious. The deployment of external labour and familial domination of management were important to employers' attempts to come to terms with the demands of an unpredictable market. Yet the vagaries of the market and the importance of the family also served to constrain management. Wary of not being able to compete during the 'busy' season, they could not simply dispense with external labour at the whim of the market. And, important though the family were, they were not always competent. It seemed as though this lack of competence had to be tolerated. These more complex views of casualisation and the role of the family do not fit neatly with their more usual presentations as mechanisms of undiluted managerial autocracy in accounts of minority enterprise. Ostensibly 'rational' responses to the market pressures developed their own tensions and uncertainties, which management had to accommodate. If management did attempt to accommodate such pressures through autocracy and 'direct control', a successful outcome was not assured. The next section follows the progress of an order being processed in company A and duly illustrates the 'dysfunctionality' of managerial coercion.

The Cost of Close Control

According to Gee orders were taken by members of the family without fully realising the implications that they had for production,

" Only I really know if we can really make the garment and what the problems are, yet I'm not consulted when it comes to deciding whether or not to take the order."

Gee had a point. This reluctance to inform Gee about orders taken (usually by Phu or Bas) stemmed partly from rank bad management, that is, poor communication. A more significant explanation, however, would seem to be an assertion of managerial prerogative by Phu and Bas despite the fact an exercise of it in this context had often proved dysfunctional. They did not really know enough about the logistics of garment production to give unequivocal responses to order enquiries, yet they did so because it was their 'right'. To have involved Gee directly in this process would have been a dilution of this right.

On a particular occasion, Phu accepted an order, a small and difficult order from a quality-conscious customer, without consulting Gee. Phu gave a sample of the order to Gee and then instructed him to commence production. For Gee, commencing production would, ideally, have meant that he was given the time to adjust the patterns, cut a single sample from these patterns, get a machinist to sew it up and then assess whether it matched up to the sample provided by the customer. Only after this process (which takes one and a half days) had been successfully completed would Gee ordinarily start to produce the order in earnest.

The order was placed on 3.4.90, to be completed by 3.5.90. This was ample time, but Gee was not informed about it until 20.4.90. Time was running out. Phu instructed Gee to start production immediately without Gee having a chance to produce a sample garment. Gee duly did this, but it soon transpired that the garments, which had all been cut now, were oversized. Once this problem had come to light (which was at the sewing stage) production was stopped. There then followed an intense period of negotiation with the customer, who agreed that the problem could be solved by a certain gerrymandering of the sizes. Two days were lost.

Once this had been sorted out, the machinists (Luk and Nat) were asked to get the garments out as quickly as possible. They were not particularly happy at producing this garment in the first place since it was complex and they could not secure a satisfactory piece-rate on standard garments. They were put on day-rate but the amount that was eventually agreed was not as much as they would get if they were working on piece-rate. The pressure on Phu and the unsatisfactory level of the day-rate meant that they were intent on getting the order out of the way as quickly as possible so that they could get back on to piece-rate work.

After the garments had been sewn, they went to the packers, who were responsible for checking them, removing loose threads and packing. They too were under intense pressure, which took the form of Phu physically standing over them to 'get the garments out'. The entire order was rejected. The customer claimed, rightly, that the stitching was faulty and that there were loose threads on the garments. Gee presented the garments to Phu, who then asserted that

" The bloody cutting, what a mess. Nat - he doesn't know how to make anything; and the packers, the bastards, I stood over them and told them to look out for these things. "

Despite these assertions, at every stage of the production process of this particular garment, Phu exercised fairly direct control, and it proved disastrous. The point was not lost on Gee, " Phu's on everyone's back so they get through it however they can. This is what happens."

Some of the processes evident in this example from company A, notably the dysfunctionality of close supervision, were particular features in Gouldner's classic study of a gypsum plant (1954). Gouldner focused upon the dynamics of workplace relations in a factory that changed from a personalised mode of control to a much more bureaucratic and 'rational' form of organisation. Under conditions of personalised managerial control (which was labelled the 'indulgency pattern'), workplace relations were decentralised, flexible and informal. There was a high degree of 'trust' and workers were motivated. However, the stability of this pattern of social relations was disrupted by changes in the local community and the product market.

Against the background of a declining rural community in the midst of economic rationalisation and an industrial sector encountering increasing competition, management were encouraged to move to a more formal and bureaucratic system of organisation. Accordingly, the norms and customs of the indulgency pattern soon dissipated as management endeavoured to operate in a more 'rational' manner. The employment relationship came to be viewed in narrow economic terms. The outcome was discontent, disillusionment and industrial action. This move to bureaucracy occasioned a more calculative response from workers and a greater awareness of the terms of the effort bargain, a response that led to lower levels of performance. Management attempted to counteract this 'problem' through closer supervision. However, close supervision increased the visibility of power relations within the factory and duly raised tensions between management and workers to such an extent that strike action was taken. The underlying stability and flexibility provided by the indulgency pattern had been destroyed and replaced by fragile set of relationships that were extremely brittle.

Management, then, had a 'logic' to rationalise. The increasingly volatile nature of the product and labour markets seemed to be pushing them in the direction of greater efficiency which, it was thought, could best be achieved through bureaucratic means. However, when they attempted to operationalise this logic at the level of the workplace, it had unintended consequences which militated against the 'rationality' and efficiency that management sought.

Gouldner's study highlights how the dynamics of bureaucratisation necessitated closer supervision and, in doing so, proved dysfunctional. The message seems to be that it was this move to bureaucratise, this progression towards to a more 'rational' form of organisation that precipitated the 'problem'. Implicit in this suggestion appears to be the notion that if the 'problems' of bureaucracy could be ironed out, then dysfunctionality would not necessarily ensue. In other words, if the politics of management or the agency issue were to be adequately resolved, labour control would not prove so problematic. This view, however, minimises the contradictory role of management. The example drawn from company A illustrates the point that even in the absence of bureaucracy, the contradictions and tensions involved in managing labour are many and varied.

The market that company A were in was exerting particular pressures. In an attempt to accommodate these pressures management, on this occasion, exercised fairly direct control. This took the form of prescribing tight deadlines on Gee, the imposition of a day-rate over Luk and Nat and the close supervision of the packers.

Such an approach, although ostensibly 'rational', went against the grain of existing customs and understandings at play on the shopfloor. Gee, for example, could have produced the patterns to the appropriate specifications; he had done so on many occasions with other garments. However, in this instance, it was virtually impossible for him to produce the required patterns to the required standard in the time available. Moreover, the fact that his expert opinion was ignored for the sake of alacrity was a further disincentive to engage his abilities in the necessarily time-consuming task of producing a proper pattern.

In the case of Luk and Nat, by imposing a rate, Phu effectively ignored the fluidities involved in the setting of the piece-rate. Chapter four discusses the rate-fixing process in detail; but, in essence, it was characterised by bargaining, politicking and negotiation. Time constraints had pressurised Phu into by-passing such intricacies and setting a rate that Luk and Nat regarded as an unfair reflection on their abilities. The outcome was a garment that they deemed appropriate to the level of reward and time available for production rather than a product fit for the market.

Finally, in relation to the packers, Phu's constant physical presence was designed to get them to pack as many garments as possible. However, they were also responsible for spotting defects in the garments and any loose threads that would detract from the appearance of the products. Given the often intimidating nature of the supervision exercised by Phu, it was rational for them to expedite the packing element of their work as quickly as possible without spending too much time on the lengthier processes of fault detection.

This example highlights the irrationalities and cost of close supervision. Forces emanating from the market pressurised management into acting in more 'rational' manner leading to closer supervision of the workforce. As Gouldner demonstrated in his study, this approach had unintended consequences and ultimately proved dysfunctional. However, the dysfunctionality was not, as in Gouldner's study, a consequence of the problems of bureacracy or the agency issue. Rather, it exemplifed the contradictory role of management in the capital-labour relation.

Conclusion

The concern of this chapter was to provide an insight into how management in the West Midlands clothing sector handles uncertainty stemming primarily from the market. Within the general debates on the nature of management, the management of uncertainty has rightly come to be regarded as crucial to understanding the dynamics of workplace relations. However, the concrete ways in which management comes to terms with its increasingly volatile and unpredictable environment has attracted rather less attention.

The received image of management in West Midlands clothing firms seems to be one of brutal bosses exercising harsh control over an often vulnerable workforce. The vulnerability or otherwise of workers will be considered in the following chapters, but the evidence from the current study suggests that the 'rationality' of management implicit in such categorisations is subject to question.

It was undoubtedly the case that manufacturers in the West Midlands faced extreme pressures from a number of sources, particularly the market. Customers, whether they were chainstores, wholesalers or larger manufacturers, were fickle, imposed onerous conditions and displayed precious little loyalty. These pressures were compounded by a lack of management training, poor design and the practices of fabric suppliers. Manufacturers, locked into this industry by the absence of opportunity elsewhere, had to accommodate these pressures, but it did not necessarily follow that they did so by exercising autocratic management. The form that the response has taken is widely believed to be the casualisation and intensification of labour, and this is usually considered indicative of harsh management. Evidence from the current study seriously questions such assertions by pointing to the complexities inherent within these processes.

Although casualisation was evident in most firms, this did not necessarily lead to a 'hire and fire' situation. External labour was sought because its utilisation was seen by many as the only way in which production could be increased to meet surges in demand. However, it did not always follow that once demand had been satisfied, the services of the external labour would be peremptorily abandoned. The unpredictability of the market meant that manufacturers were often very wary of letting external labour go, even when there were no concrete orders.

The process of casualisation therefore highlighted the contradictory position of management. Management utilised external labour to cope with the surges and the slumps in the market. External labour afforded employers a certain flexibility with which they could respond to the demands of the market. However, management often found themselves unable to fully exploit this flexibility because they needed to retain external labour during the quieter times in order to be in a position where they could compete when there was an up-turn. The result was a state of continual ambiguity as management tried to balance the demands of a rapidly fluctuating product market with the need to keep labour supplied with work.

In terms of the organisation of production at the level of the workplace, the findings were not consistent with an intensification of labour scenario. The organisation of the shopfloor and issues around the effort bargain are explored in chapters four and five; the concern here was the use of familial labour in management. Familial labour was integral to the organisation of the workplace. Family members held key positions within the firm and in doing so, made the process of supervision easier and cheaper. Where family members were absent, as in the case of company A, social relations were markedly different as management simultaneously endeavoured to harness the creative capacities of key workers while also seeking to diminish their influence. However, contrary to the impression given in existing accounts of the clothing industry, familial labour can also serve as a considerable constraint upon management. Examples from companies A and C illustrated the extent to which the family acted as a brake upon management 'rationality'.

The capacity of the family to frustrate as well as facilitate managerial autocracy again brings into focus the contradictions facing management. Familial members' pervasiveness within the firms was a major resource for management. However, the need to preserve the family within the firm prevented the full fruits of this policy from being achieved. Incompetence, indiscipline and indolence were no bar from familial involvement within the firm, but they were a constraint upon management 'rationality'.

In managing market uncertainty then, the casualisation of work and the deployment of family labour were important mechanisms used by employers in the West Midlands clothing industry, but the processes inherent in such tactics were not as simple nor autocratic as commonly portrayed. They highlight the point that even ostensibly 'rational' policies will have uncertain outcomes, and in doing so, provide a clear illustration of the contradictory nature of management. Furthermore, such policies generate further uncertainties that have to be managed. The next chapter explores the uncertainties arising from the shopfloor.

4

Shopfloor Organisation

This chapter assesses the way in which work was organised on the shopfloor. In doing so, it will inevitably concentrate on the machinists, who comprised the bulk of the workforce. To this end, it will be necessary to consider the forces that determined how and why and workers ended up in this type of firm and the complex and often conflicting pressures that shaped the production process.

In many clothing-based studies, Westwood, Hoel and Rainnie for example, the general plight of the machinists in the workplace is discussed but the actual organisation of the shopfloor has received relatively little attention. Considerable evidence of the extent of worker subordination is presented in these accounts: workers are subjected to harsh management regimes, discretion is limited and their scope for exercising influence is negligible. But the actual system of production, and the ways in which management and workers shape it, is not really examined.

Westwood's account of the labour process in one of the departments within 'Stitchco' gives the impression that management were in control of the production process despite the fact that the machinists had 'responsibilities to other members of the unit to maintain the flow of production' (1984: 18). Management's inability to co-ordinate the sectionalised production system often led to 'delays and frustrations', but it appeared that the women were the only ones who suffered as a result of this managerial incompetence. Individual machinists had no control over the nature of their tasks and management seemed to insist on their being 'flexible'. The women 'protested at being moved around' (p20) but the actual form that this protest took is not considered. There were general acts of 'resistance' evident in the fiddles, 'foreigners' and celebrations that the women engaged in, but their connection to the production process is not made explicit and why an otherwise coercive management tolerated such actions was not explained.

Although Hoel briefly alludes to the division of labour in her study of clothing firms in Coventry, she fails to consider the nature of shopfloor organisation. We are told that the 'skilled' work, usually the cutting duties, were performed by men while the 'semi-skilled' and 'unskilled' tasks were carried out by women (1982: 83-84). There is no explanation of the dynamics of the production process and the mutual dependence of management and workers. The emphasis seems to be on the severe nature of the management regime and the way in which facets of Asian culture buttressed employer domination.

Rainnie barely mentions the production process at all. Owner-managers of clothing companies found themselves in a dependent relationship with the chainstores, which it is argued, virtually obliged them to bear down on the workforce: 'one effect of dependency is a pronounced diminution of the freedom of movement open to the individual owner-manager of small clothing factories. What is produced, under what conditions and for how much are strictly laid down. Not only is management restricted in its options, but these self same restrictions mean that little or no interference, from the workforce, can be tolerated' (1989: 99). Within the workplace, the result is an 'authoritarian management system' which workers have little opportunity to influence.

By providing an insight into the nature of shopfloor organisation in the clothing firms within the current study, this chapter aims to address some of these deficiencies and offer an alternative interpretation.

The first of two sections explains how workers ended up in the clothing industry, that is, why they 'chose' to work in such firms. As in the case of Asian entrepreneurs, the operation of discrimination within mainstream employment is integral to any explanation of the preponderance of Asians in this sector of the economy. The way in which they entered the clothing industry, the recruitment process, and its association with 'training' will then be discussed since it encouraged particular kinds of workers.

Having assessed the processes by which workers found themselves in the clothing industry, the discussion will then focus on what they actually do. The second section looks at the organisation of work on the shopfloor. After noting the division of labour in typical clothing companies, the actual system of production will be considered. It is clearly a much more complex question than individual workers simply making garments. Having examined the method of production, the ways in which work is allocated will then be discussed. This process is not just a question of matching work to skill, it is a complex affair mediated by factors like the nature of the product market, the labour market, culture and caste.

Entry into Work

The previous chapter noted the large extent to which the Asian community dominated the clothing industry in the West Midlands. It is estimated that the sector accounts for the employment of some 30,000 workers, the majority of whom are Asian women employed as machinists (WMPLU, 1991). The findings of the current study support this general picture. At the survey stage, it was evident that women comprised the vast bulk of the workforce, numbering 243 out of a total of 289. Moreover, 276 of these employees were of Asian ethnic origin, with a total of 246 actually born in India.

Phizacklea (1990) contends that the position of minority women in clothing firms within the secondary sector of fashionwear production can only be understood within the broader context of racism and sexism. Racism and sexism were enshrined in British immigration legislation. The Commonwealth Immigrants Act of 1962, which was essentially a measure to curb the number of black people entering this country, meant that most minority women, particularly Asian women, entered after that date as 'family' women or on a voucher sponsored by a relative in business. Hence, rather than recognising women as free workers, 'British immigration law has been framed on the assumption that women are the chattels of men' (p96). The constraints imposed by immigration legislation were compounded by the pervasiveness of racial discrimination in employment.

In attempting to explain why so many Asians turned to the clothing industry, one must again look at the unfavourable opportunity structure that faced many black workers. As with the rise of the ethnic business sector discussed in chapter one, it would seem that it was discrimination in mainstream employment rather than the possession of any 'cultural flair' that largely accounted for the preponderance of Asians in this sector of the economy. This was certainly evident from discussions with machinists in the case study companies. They gave similar reasons for entering the clothing industry. Below are some of their comments.

"I can't speak English, everyone here is so friendly, and coming from India, it did not seem too alien an environment. "

" I've never been to work for anyone else. I don't know about the world outside, whether they're good or bad or what they pay. I came into clothing because everyone else did it. "

" Sewing was all that was available. "

" Sewing was the only thing that I could get into. "

" I had to go wherever the work was. It was the only job that I could get. "

" I tried to find a job elsewhere after college but was not successful, so I came here because my Mum worked here. "

" I did not like sewing but I could not get a job anywhere else. "

Lack of choice occasioned by a combination of discrimination and ignorance of the wider labour market explains why so many Asian women turned to the clothing industry. As the comments indicate, these workers felt that they would stand little chance of securing work in mainstream employment despite the fact that many would have liked such an opportunity. Their choices were severely limited and, for many, the only option seemed to be to work in ethnic enterprise in the form of Asian-owned clothing companies. Moreover, clothing employers wanted Asian (that is, cheap) labour, and workers turning to such companies did not have to go through interviews or other formal recruitment procedures.

Recruitment

Employers in the survey stage of the study, without exception, used the word of mouth method of recruitment. Two firms had advertised in the past, but not with any real degree of success. The grapevine was still the most effective system of recruitment. Generally, the process entailed the proprietor asking his workers to encourage friends and relatives to come to work for him (and it was invariably him). The whole process was very informal, with no firms using application forms or interviews. These particular channels of recruitment made it more likely that the workers recruited would be Asian.

The recruitment of raw trainees was rare. Owners appeared only to be interested in skilled machinists. There was no formal induction programme and the recruits would be slotted into production almost immediately.

The overwhelming majority of firms were experiencing difficulties in recruiting skilled sewing machinists. However, the notion of a 'labour shortage' in this context needs to be inspected more closely since it was much more than simply a question of a scarcity of workers ready and willing to do the job of a machinist. Many owners attributed this 'labour shortage' to an unwillingness on the part of the younger generation of Asian women to take up such work. It was more than a question of money, rather, the opportunity for social contact was limited in such places. One manufacturer summed it up in the following manner, " The younger generation like to have a chat and don't like to be locked up." The message seemed to be that there was a shortage of a particular kind of labour, namely pliant, cheap immigrant labour.

Hoel, Rainnie and Phizacklea (1990) all claim that a major reason why management was able to act in a harsh, indeed brutal manner towards their workforce was due to the availability of a pool of cheap, usually female labour. If recent survey evidence is correct (Lewis, 1988; Mawson, 1988), then this pool of labour has all but dried up. Clothing manufacturers in the West Midlands are experiencing a shortage of skilled labour, a point that was emphatically confirmed at the survey stage. The heavily gender-laden view of what constitutes a 'skilled' worker in the context of the clothing industry has been addressed elsewhere (Coyle, 1982), but the point that needs to be stressed is that the labour shortage is not a shortage per se but a shortage of cheap immigrant labour.

Training

The problematic notion of 'labour shortage' was further illustrated when the employers' view of training in relation to the machinists was examined. Despite the apparent dearth of skilled labour, few employers trained workers in any systematic or developmental way. The employment of trainees was rare and the existence of anything resembling a training strategy was rarer still. Had employers adopted a training policy, the problem of skill shortages would have been less acute since the apparent shortage was not due to a scarcity of workers with the ability to work as machinists. In Birmingham for example, which has the largest number of clothing firms in the West Midlands, unemployment in October 1990 was 10.9% compared to a national average of 5.9%. Moreover, in particular inner city areas where garment manufacturers tend to be clustered, like Handsworth (21%) and Sparkbrook (23.4%), the position was even more stark (Birmingham City Council, 1990). Rather than a shortage of labour, it was the conditions of economic uncertainty under which employers operated that made it improbable that they would invest in training.

Nevertheless, of the employers interviewed, only two stated that they did not train their staff. However, the 'training' that the other owners spoke of was more akin to a probationary or trial period than any form of progressive training. New recruits were given a period of time in which they could 'prove' themselves. The shortest period was a day, the longest was fourteen days. In this time, they would have to become proficient enough to earn themselves a 'decent wage' on piece-rate. Usually the supervisor would 'train' them during this period, but in most cases, they would be put on the production line almost immediately.

The rate of pay during this period ranged from nothing (the proprietor of this particular company claimed that he was 'doing the machinists a favour by giving them a chance to train') to £80 per week. Most companies paid a nominal wage of between £30-£40 per week.

It was clear that this period was used, by workers and management alike, as a means of assessing the extent to which they could 'fit' into the existing system of production. Management, ostensibly desperate for machinists, nevertheless had to take on board such considerations as the level of skill of the machinist, where she would fit into the pattern of production, her willingness to perform a range of operations, 'speed', compatibility with the other machinists and so on. Potential recruits had to weigh up whether they wanted to work 'on' or 'off' the books, the attitude of management and whether or not they could get on with fellow workers. These factors were important in explaining the apparent longevity of tenure of machinists in case study companies' B and C, as the following comments of workers indicate;

> " I like my friends here and it is quite near my house. The children are at school locally so when I'm needed, I just go. The bosses don't mind."

> " I like working here because the women are good, I can do what I want and they [management] pick me up in the mornings and drop me off in the evenings. "

> " I like it here, it's nice. We come here when we want, we go when we want and work as hard as we want. "

> " I live nearby and have children so I have to leave during work hours sometimes. The bosses don't mind. "

" The management talk to us nicely and the work is the same everywhere. "

The complexity of the labour shortage issue was further exemplified in company C. The managing director claimed that by far his most pressing problem was the shortage of skilled machinists. He stated that he had to rely increasingly on sub-contractors to meet production targets and found himself in a position where he had to extend delivery times or turn away business because of this inability to recruit a sufficient number of machinists. Yet, despite this apparent shortage, it was revealed that between 25 and 40 new recruits were taken on every year but almost invariably left after a week or two.

This apparently contradictory situation was not simply a consequence of management weeding out unsuitable workers. Rather, the outcome was again the product of a two-way process. Some of the recruits did not want to work 'on the books' and others, so the supervisor claimed, 'did not like the work' or 'just couldn't sew'. Many, therefore, left of their own accord. However, the last two remarks by the supervisor were revealing. 'Not liking the work' was an indication that the type of work that these recruits were given was neither easy nor lucrative. This was not surprising given the fact that most of the machinists in this company had been there for over ten years and had developed their own systems of working and task allocation. Similarly, the reference to some recruits not being able to sew could have been a reflection of the machinists' particular pattern of production as much as the proficiency of the recruit.

The process of recruitment and 'training' in companies were, then, highly informal with little evidence of bureaucracy or formal procedure. Workers were involved in attracting potential recruits to the firm and were seen by management as perhaps the most important means of enlisting new labour. In large part, informality in recruitment through the use of family, community and workforce connections has often been viewed as a means of furthering management's control over the workforce (Dick and Morgan, 1987: Hoel, 1982: Jenkins, 1986: Brooks and Singh, 1979).

In their study of a textile mill, for example, Dick and Morgan (1987) found that a family ideology within the firm was an important element in securing the flexibility required to operate in a highly competitive sector. Employers sought certain qualities like 'reliability' and 'conformity', qualities which could be guaranteed through family contacts and family discipline. Hoel's study also highlights the benefits of such contacts to management. Hoel found that

" In so far as jobs were obtained through family and community connections, there were obligations to accept the job as such. It would not do to complain about the terms and conditions of employment, in part because this would reflect badly on those who introduced the women to the employer " (1982: 82).

The utility to management of features like stability and discipline are beyond doubt and help to explain the continued prevalence of informal recruitment practices, even in large organisations (Collinson et al, 1990; Maguire, 1988). However, informality can have unintended consequences which may militate against the stability that informal recruitment is supposed to provide. In the context of the current study for example, by allowing the workforce so much autonomy in attracting new workers, management were effectively ceding considerable discretion over eventual recruitment decisions. Many of the machinists from the case study companies had been with the firms for a number of years. They had developed their own norms, understandings and patterns of working. Given the dynamics of the production system, it would have been extremely difficult for new recruits to survive for any length of time unless they fitted into existing ways of working. The high turnover of trainees in company C in the midst of an apparent 'labour shortage' bears testimony to this. To use Jenkins' (1986) point regarding 'suitability' and 'acceptability', it was evident that newcomers to the firms needed to be 'suitable' in the technical sense of being able to sew, and 'acceptable' in terms of being able to 'fit in' - but 'acceptable' at least as much to workers as to management.

The potential for such a situation to generate tensions was evident. Chapter six provides examples where technically competent recruits, enlisted by management, were not allowed to stay because they were not of the same background as the core of long-serving employees within the existing workforce. These long-serving workers manipulated the productive process so as to effectively starve them of work. The decision to recruit, then, could not be made on the basis of concepts like 'efficiency' or productivity alone. The nature of a production process heavily influenced by the existing workforce had to be taken into account. It is to this production system that the discussion will now turn.

Work Organisation

The Production Process

The division of labour in the kind of clothing companies investigated here tended to be quite similar. The 'skilled' jobs, namely those of lay-planning and cutting, were held by men who were usually the employers themselves or relatives. Although it is sometimes argued that men perform these functions because it requires strength, Coyle's (1982) point that these jobs are regarded as skilled because men classify them as such seems much more credible. Furthermore, as discussed in chapter one, family domination of these functions was an important means of securing some kind of control over the production process as well as saving on cost. Where it was absent, as in the case of company A, social relations were noticeably different.

The least skilled jobs usually involved packing, clipping loose threads off the garments and the storing of the merchandise. In the three case study companies, the tasks were performed by a variety of people. In company A, there were three men responsible for these functions, all of whom were Asians visiting this country in order to see friends and relatives. Not surprisingly, the turnover of such workers in this firm was quite high. According to one of the more permanent of the firm's employees, they were all 'visitors'. In companies B and C, this type of work tended to be performed by older women who could no longer earn a decent wage sewing on piece-rate. These workers were the least well-rewarded category of employees despite the fact that they were charged with one of the most important functions, that of checking the quality of the jackets. This category of worker could often find themselves involved in a bewildering array of activities. For example, during the 'quiet' season, the packers from company A were instructed to assist in the renovation of the proprietor's newly-acquired house.

In company C, two such workers were employed on undoubtedly dangerous tasks. The firm had a laminating machine. Basically, this machine glued polyester filling to lining material which serves to create the padding effect in padded jackets. Adhesive is sprayed on to the lining material, which revolves around a roller, and is then attached to the polyester, which is on another roller. The stench of the glue was quite oppressive, yet the two workers operating the machine did not wear gloves, masks or any other form of protection. To the side of the machine lay three empty containers. The labels on the containers warned that the adhesive contained a harmful product called dichloromethane and, therefore, should not be inhaled. I was there for ten minutes before my eyes became sore and breathing became difficult. I asked one of the workers why he did not wear any protective equipment. " It's too much hassle ", came the reply.

Such workers, then, were probably the most vulnerable of those engaged in the companies investigated. Their tenure was usually brief, they could be asked to do almost anything, they were very poorly paid and subject to the closest supervision. In company C for example, everyone was employed 'on the books' apart from three 'general assistants'. Within company A, the treatment of such workers was harsh and extremely arbitrary. They too were paid 'off the books', they worked a six day week (9.00 - 7.30 were the average working hours) and were often verbally abused. Three such workers who had been with the firm for over six months before Christmas were told, over the telephone, that they would no longer be needed in the new year.

Then there were the machinists. The job of a machinist tends to be classified as 'semi-skilled' (Coyle, 1982), but in most typical clothing firms in the West Midlands, the actual sewing of the garment is probably one of the most complex and demanding tasks that there is. The sewing machine is but a power-operated needle which produces a series of stitches continuously. All the rest is left to the operator. The operator controls the size of the stitch, the tension of the sewing threads and the rate of stitch formation. She controls the shape of the sewing line and hence the shape of the finished garment, as well as the matching and fitting of one ply against another. Furthermore, she must interpret instructions on a work ticket about different styles, have the knowledge to thread up a machine correctly (often a highly complex process), and be able to judge acceptable quality during and after the operations. Hence the operations in clothing manufacture are largely machinist-controlled (Carr and Latham, 1988).

The actual task of sewing occupies about one-fifth of the time of the average sewing operation. The other four-fifths of the time is spent on activities such as preparing the fabric to be sewn, trimming, folding, creasing, marking and disposal after sewing and bundling. Although these activities are sometimes referred to as 'ancillary handling', they constitute the core of the typical clothing operation, and they have not been mechanised to any significant extent (Carr and Latham, 1988).

The job of a machinist is, therefore, a complex one involving judgement, skill and dexterity. However, the machinists were not an undifferentiated group of workers: there were divisions between them based on tasks and functions. To understand the basis of these divisions, it is necessary to have an appreciation of how the system of production operated on the shopfloor.

A sectionalised production process was in place in all the companies studied. In this way, machinists specialised in producing a particular part of a garment rather than the garment as a whole. Hence, one machinist would concentrate on pockets, whilst another will sew the linings and so on. Within company B, this process of specialisation was around five stages:

Stage 1 - Trimmings (Collars and belts)
Stage 2 - Pockets
Stage 3 - Linings
Stage 4 - Zips
Stage 5 - Finishing

The different stages were not equally complex; they required varying degrees of skill. The simplest task, for example, was that of the linings, which was essentially a question of sewing straight seams. The most complex tasks tended to be the making of pockets and the finishing of garments, both of which demanded more complicated manoeuvres and stitching. Consequently, the pocket hands and the finishers tended to be the better rewarded machinists. It was these categories of machinists that were most scarce.

For this type of production system to operate 'efficiently', it was necessary not only to have a continuous supply of work, but a continuous supply of 'appropriate' work. There had to be enough pockets, linings, zips, trimmings and so on to keep the differently skilled machinists continually occupied. The task of organising this work, moreover, was not entirely in the hands of management. Making a garment was a sequential process insofar as it went through a number of distinct stages. Hence pocket hands were unable start their particular operations until the trimmings had been attached by the previous machinists; the linings could not be sewn until the pockets had been completed; and so on. Management were dependent on machinists to work in such a way as to ensure that operatives kept each other supplied with work so that the line flowed smoothly.

Not only did management rely on workers to manage the flow line, there seemed to be an expectation that machinists should also remedy problems in production that stemmed from a lack of managerial competence. On numerous occasions I witnessed the cutters in the three case study companies asking machinists to 'deal' with problems like faulty cutting, poor design and bad planning. They would ask operatives, for example, to trim poorly cut fabric manually, shorten a zip if it was too long and manipulate the fabric so that flaws in the material would not show up on the finished product. An incident from company A further demonstrates this point.

Luk and Nat, two highly experienced machinists, were complaining to me about the cutting of the garments. They had to manipulate fabric where it was incorrectly cut so that the final product appeared neat. Furthermore, they had to remedy design problems that neither Phu, the proprietor, nor Gee, the cutter, originally anticipated. For example, a rally jacket that they were working on was all white with a narrow purple strip around the middle. After a few garments had been made, it was apparent that the seam of the purple strip was visible beneath the white material. This gave the garment an untidy appearance and probably would have been rejected by the customer. Nat and Luk were now expected to come up with a means of remedying this problem.

Despite the significant extent to which management were dependent on workers' skills to address production problems, the logic of the productive system was such that machinists should endeavour to complete their individual operation as quickly as possible. Sometimes, this proved dysfunctional. On one occasion in company B, the joiner forgot to affix a cuff on a partially completed garment that she had passed on to the next machinist down the line, the finisher. The finisher noticed that the cuff was missing but continued her operation rather than return the garment to the joiner to put on the cuff. This effectively meant that the completed garment had one cuff missing and therefore, was not acceptable. Since the 'fault' lay with the joiner, she had to rectify the mistake. Remedying this error was not simply a question of adding on an extra cuff. Since the cuff could only be sewn from inside the sleeve, the garment had to be unpicked before the cuff could be inserted. Commenting on this incident, Sig stated that 'it's like someone putting a wheel on a car without a tyre. You're going to have to take the wheel back off in order to put the tyre on'. Sig claimed that many machinists 'plodded on ignoring the faults'.

The tensions generated by management's lack of command over the production process and reliance on the capacity of workers to organise the shopfloor occasioned considerable uncertainty. Management faced an array of pressures from the market which could only be accommodated by the active effort of workers on the shopfloor. The deployment of such effort was a matter of negotiation, formal and informal, rather than direction. Gel of company C summed up the extent to which management relinquished its grasp over the direction of production once work was in progress,

> "We have to pay the ladies every week whether or not we can get the order out. Once the work enters this room, we can't really plan. Some of the machinists might take work home, some might not. They might be sick, they might take time off, they might come in late. If there are six lines on the go, we can't be sure which one will be finished first or when it will be completed. You just can't predict your workforce."

In spite of the fragmented nature of the system of production in the case study firms, management, then, still had to harness the expertise of workers in order to address problems in production that they themselves were not really competent to handle. However, they also needed to direct workers' efforts to some extent in order to ensure that the company could compete. The previous chapter noted the increasingly uncertain and volatile nature of the market that these firms operated in. Intense competition, fickle customers, tight delivery times, rapid changes in fashion and the seasonal nature of the industry contributed to the creation of a high degree of uncertainty. Management responded to these pressures in complex and contradictory ways, not by simply intensifying and casualising labour as some have argued. Nevertheless, employers in this sector have to adapt to survive and so, it seems, do workers who, like their bosses, are locked into this type of industry by racism in its various manifestations. As Gel of company C put it,

> "We've got no choice, they've got no choice. If we're going to get the orders, then we have to accept these changes. The women realise this and accept it. They've been working here for 10 years and understand that. We don't really force them."

Work Allocation

Workers, like employers, like to have long runs of particular lines. Specialisation on a particular product allows the opportunity to develop speed and therefore increase earnings. However, they too have to accommodate the pressures of surviving in a ferociously competitive market.

When respondents to the survey stage of the study were asked how work was allocated, they all claimed that it was distributed on the basis of skill. Hence when, for example, the pocket hand finished her work, she would be given pockets, when the linings operative completed her batch, she would be provided with more linings. Evidence derived from the case studies, however, suggests that the real picture was much more complicated. The allocation of work cannot be separated from the market, yet it would be mistaken to claim that it was shaped solely by it. Although machinists had their specialisms and preferences, the allocation of work was a complex, contested and contingent affair.

The most obvious effect of these pressures was on the type of work that they were engaged upon. Although operatives in companies B and C claimed that they were kept 'busy' most of the time, it was not necessarily on the same task. They had to switch jobs, and when they did, the result was often a drop in earnings. Machinists in both of these companies were asked what happened when their particular work ran short.

Company B:

MACHINIST 1 - Finisher.
When her particular job, which is finishing, has been completed, she is moved to a different job, usually pockets. "I don't like to be put on pockets but I have to change, there's no choice. " She is moved every four or five weeks to pockets, on which she remains for about a week. Whilst on pockets, she claims that her 'money goes down by a lot [£20]'. With the order currently in progress, she has been on pockets for three weeks.

MACHINIST 2 - Pocket hand.
She is switched to 'other jobs' every three or four days and remains on them for two or three days, " Until the order goes through and is completed, I can't have any more pockets. " Her money also drops by around £20 whilst on other work.

MACHINIST 3 - Joining
She is moved to belts, cuffs, collars and basically whatever is required. She does not enjoy these other jobs and claims that she has to do them. She loses between £20 and £25 whist on these jobs.

MACHINIST 4 - Pocket hand. She is transferred to finishing after every two weeks of being on pockets. She loses around £10, but contends, "There's nothing that we can do about it, we just have a moan between ourselves. "

MACHINIST 5 - Pocket hand
She moves to either joining or finishing. She switches every two weeks or so, performing the new job for a week. Her money goes down by about £20, " If I did mind, it would make no difference, you have to do it. "

MACHINIST 6 - Linings
"I go home when work is short, but it doesn't really bother me. I just come here to pass the time. One week I took home £3 and I didn't mind at all. Sometimes I only come in for a chat. "

MACHINIST 7 - Overlocker
When the overlocking work has finished, she is moved to an ordinary lockstitch machine. For every six weeks on an overlocker, she will spend a week on an ordinary machine and her earnings will drop by around £20 as a consequence.

Company C

MACHINIST 1 - Pocket hand
" I don't get enough pockets. I work on pockets for three or four weeks, then I work on other jobs like lining and joining for three or four weeks." Whilst working on these other jobs, her earnings drop by around £15.

MACHINIST 2 - Linings
When lining work is not available, she is transferred to joining and finishing. For the past six months, she has been on day-rate. This has meant that her earnings have dropped by around £10.

MACHINIST 3 - Linings When lining work is not available, she is transferred to zips and joining. It is more difficult to do these other jobs so she is put on a day-rate. However, her earnings still drop by around £10.

MACHINIST 4 - Collars
She is moved to any other work that may need doing, and she does this one week in every four. When she is on this other work, she is paid on a day rate basis of £1.80 per hour, " I don't like day-rate, I like to earn my own money. "

MACHINIST 5 - Finishing
She is switched to other work and paid on a day-rate basis of £2.11 per hour. She does not like day-rate work but, 'you have to do it, they [management] can't help it if the work has finished'.

The process of job allocation in companies B and C highlighted the extent to which the impact of the market influenced the work of the machinists. They were kept 'busy' for most of the year seemingly irrespective of the state of the company's order book. However, they were expected to cope with the diversity and rapidity of fashion changes despite incurring a loss of earnings in the process. The inevitability of fashion changes did not necessarily mean that job switches on the shopfloor were accepted unquestioningly by workers on a day-to-day basis. For example, on a particular occasion in company B, the favoured work of a highly skilled machinist, Sian, had run out. The supervisor, Dor, asked Sian to sew some garments that were regarded as 'difficult' for a short while. Sian complained that she could not sew the garments, but Dor refused to allocate her any other work. The result was that Sian walked out. According to Sig, a partner in company B, Sian had acted hastily,

> " She left without saying anything to anyone. The old women [more experienced machinists] would not have let her go, they would have sorted it out. We [management] would not have let her go, we would have pacified her somehow."

The following morning, Sig, together with two machinists, went to Sian's home in order to persuade her to come back to work. According to one of the   machinists,

> " We went to ask why she came home, why she didn't tell us since we would have sorted it out. We would have sorted Dor out too."

Sian came back to work and on her return, was given work that she was accustomed to.

The location of the machinists' work stations in company B further illustrated how workers influenced the organisation of the shopfloor. For the sectionalised production system to operate 'efficiently', it would have been rational to place the machines according to the stages of garment production in order to ensure that the work flowed smoothly. To this end, machines should have been placed in the manner illustrated in figure 1. Production, under this scenario, would start with trimmings. The work would then flow down the line to the pocket hands, joiners and finishers. It would then be taken away for packing and distribution.

The actual juxtaposition of the work stations is shown in figure 2. The somewhat web-like illustration suggests that the machines were located in accordance to precepts other than efficiency. Dor, the supervisor, explained the arrangements in the following manner, " Some people like working together, some don't. Friends and relatives don't like to part ". Consequently, partly completed work goes around the floor in a near chaotic way, with bundles of work strewn all over the floor. This can lead to mistakes since different sizes get mixed up or mislaid.

Other forms of accommodation took the form of outright refusal to make certain garments, making 'mistakes', the stockpiling of 'easy' work and so on. The nature of such accommodations will be pursued in more detail in the next chapter, but the point to note here is that despite the exigencies of the market, the technical organisation of work was a complex affair mediated by an array of factors, not just 'skill'.

This complexity can perhaps be seen more sharply in the case of company A. Company A employed very few on-site machinists, relying on sub-contractors and homeworkers for the bulk of its output. The way in which work was allocated in this firm was mediated by such considerations as the product market, the labour market, worker militancy and ethnicity. The following illustrations from the field notes demonstrate the significance of these factors.

Luk and Nat were two very experienced and highly skilled machinists who had been with the company for several years; in fact, in the case of Luk, the length of employment exceeded fifteen years. They are both employed 'off the books'. I visited them one day and asked why they were not making shell suits, a popular line at that point in the season. "The shell suits are pretty easy to make so Phu gets them done from the women outside. It's cheaper that way " (Luk). The shell suits were in great demand at the moment and, according to Nat, Phu did not seem overly concerned with their quality, " The women can get away with dodgy stitching because everyone wants the shell suits " (Nat). Both Luk and Nat tend to receive the 'difficult' jackets where customers were fairly strict about quality requirements, " We get the white man's order and he won't let us get away with anything " (Luk).

When Phu was contemplating manufacturing the shell suits, it was Nat and Luk who were given the initial batch to produce. They were given this work for three reasons. Firstly, both machinists were regarded as highly skilled, which, in this context, was a reference to the fact that they could sew a garment in its entirety. Secondly, given this level of ability, they could solve any design problems whilst sewing the garments. Once these

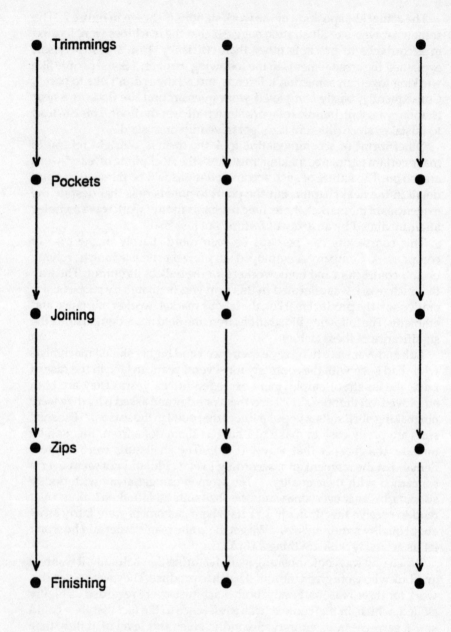

Figure 1: 'Rational' Organisation

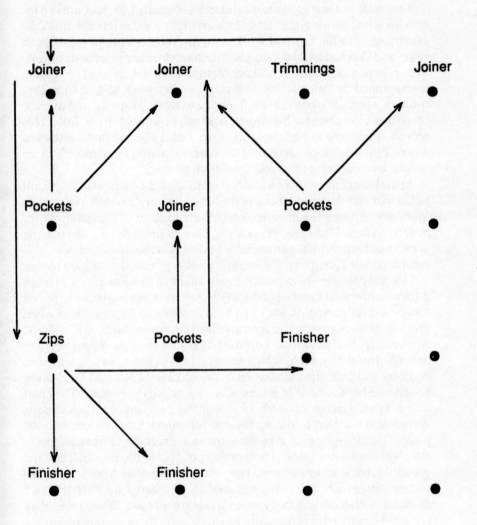

Figure 2: Actual Organisation of Machines in Company B

problems were identified and tackled, it would indeed be cheaper to give the work to 'the women outside'. Finally, Luk and Nat were given this work because of the particular nature of social relations between the two machinists and the proprietor, Phu.

As mentioned earlier, these machinists, especially Luk, had worked for Phu for some considerable time. Luk and Phu were originally from the same part of India. Luk had worked exclusively for Phu for over fifteen years and Phu had kept him supplied with work on a regular basis despite the vagaries of the market. There seemed to be a reciprocal obligation underpinned by cultural ties. Luk could expect work and, in turn, Phu could rely on Luk to be available for work, to work 'properly' and to come up with a 'fair' price for his efforts. In short, Phu could 'trust' Luk. This served effectively to tie Luk to the firm, but it also created a situation where Phu was dependent on Luk. The following example offers an insight into the nature this relationship in practice.

At the time of my visit, Luk and Nat were sewing a particularly difficult jacket that was destined for one of the firm's 'quality' English customers, Midmark. Although company A had been supplying the customer for over five years, Midmark was notorious for its small orders. The placing of orders of around 100 garments by Midmark was not uncommon. This compared with company A's average weekly production of 2000 pieces.

Luk and Nat were being asked to sew many of these smaller and more difficult orders. At the start of the week they were sewing order X, which comprised 100 garments. They had been working on it for two days when Phu asked them to stop and start another order from Midmark, order Y. Apparently, Midmark had informed Phu that they no longer wanted order X. Instead, order Y, which consisted of 40 pieces, was now urgent, and Nat and Luk were to start on it straight away. Nat and Luk, being accustomed to this state of affairs, were not unduly perturbed. They had 'come to an agreement' with Phu over the payment for such orders, demanding that they be put on day-rate for orders that were less than 100 pieces. The day-rate was to be the same as average day's work on piece-rate, 'although a few pounds here or there did not really matter. It was the principle that was important'. They claimed that they 'could not make money' otherwise. This was not something offered by Phu, it was a demand by Nat and Luk that was reluctantly conceded. Despite this, they were not happy with continually having to sew these smaller orders.

It appeared that Nat and Luk were given the orders for two reasons. Firstly, they did not appear to be as militant as other workers, " We don't make noise." They claimed that other workers were getting the longer runs and easier work because "they make a lot of noise". Secondly, they were more skilled. They claimed that other machinists weren't bothered about the garment whereas they took care to sew up a decent piece. In fact, they had to do so since the garments were for a customer that was more concerned with quality than most.

It was for these reasons that they received the 'dribs and drabs' orders from Midmark. Other machinists were more militant and not prepared to put the additional work into these elaborate garments. This effectively meant that Phu was dependent on Nat and Luk for the production of such garments, and it was this very dependency that enabled them to demand day-rate payments for such orders.

Most of the sub-contractors or units used by company A were of the same caste as the proprietor, the Kumar caste. According to Gee, who helped in the process of work allocation " It helps to be a Kumar, it gives you the edge. The sub-contractors are old-time people, they know how Phu thinks." Sometimes, this overrode economic concerns.

On one occasion, the son of one of Phu's sub-contractors quarrelled with his father and was consequently thrown out of the family home. The son turned to Phu, who gave him accommodation and a regular supply of work. The son was of the same caste as Phu, who was looked upon as a senior and a respected figure in the community. There was no real need for a machinist at that stage, and to provide work to someone who was only going to be there a short while did not appear to make economic sense. However, it appeared that Phu was under an obligation to act in the manner that he did.

These illustrations from company A highlight the complexities involved in the process of job allocation and the extent to which it was mediated by considerations like ethnicity and the product market. Clearly the relationship between Phu and Luk and other members of the same caste was one that extended beyond the cash nexus - they had obligations to each other that stemmed from caste and kinship ties. These obligations in themselves did not determine the form of the employment relationship and the process of job allocation, but they did contribute to the shaping of the outcomes. There were expectations, norms and understandings on both sides that were informed by an awareness of cultural ties as well as the exigencies of the productive system. The impact of ethnicity on the labour process is considered at greater length in chapters six and seven; the point to note here is that the 'logic' of 'rationality' was both aided and impeded by the considerations of ethnicity that obtained between Phu and Luk.

The basis of the relationship between Phu and other machinists, however, was different and ostensibly more 'rational'. With two particular machinists, who were brothers, the relationship, and therefore the process of work allocation, seemed less complicated. The brothers were regarded as 'fast' workers, just the kind that were needed to cope with surges in demand during the 'busy' season. They had no particular loyalty to the firm or the proprietor. They were there for the money, and to earn it, they needed a continuous supply of work. Phu realising how scarce workers of this kind were, duly provided it. There were no cultural ties, connections or affinities beyond the cash nexus.

Raju, on the other hand, was regarded as a 'slow' worker. He was undoubtedly skilled in the sense that he could sew a full garment, but he was not quick enough to warrant the allocation of a large amount of work and he did not possess any cultural or caste connection with Phu which may have afforded him some leeway. Moreover, he could not boost his capacity by using familial labour (as Nat did) since his wife did not sew. Consequently, he had almost to plead for work on occasions and the type of work that he did get was often the 'difficult' work usually at a rate lower than received by other machinists.

The differential treatment of the machinists in relation to job allocation is demonstrated in the following extract from the field notes:

Gee is just finishing batching up a lay of women's jackets. The allocation of this cut work is not beyond contention. The lay consists of 500 pieces. 200 will go to the brothers, 150 will be taken by Nat, Luk will receive 100 while Raju will take 50 pieces. Whilst the lay was being cut, both Nat and Raju came to the cutting table in an attempt to ensure that they would receive the work (Nat gets more because his wife sews from home). This particular job was regarded as easy, " They're like children. They see something and they want it now despite the fact that they will get the work in time " (Gee).

Raju was not confident that he would get his share. He makes his case for the 50 pieces to Gee, Bas and myself as well as Phu. He feared that the work would be given to, or taken by, the other machinists who, he claimed, were out to 'make trouble'.

The brothers, however, were assured of their work. Apparently, they had been promised at least a month's supply of this particular jacket despite the fact that Phu did not have concrete orders for the garment. Why did Phu grant them so much work ? According to Gee, the reasons were two-fold. Firstly, the brothers were regarded as 'fast' workers. Secondly, 'they make noise'. Gee claimed that the brothers insisted on having this type of garment on a regular basis. Phu acceded to these demands because machinists of this level of skill were scarce and they would be needed in the busy season.

When the 'busy' season did finally arrive the ploy of providing the brothers in company A with guaranteed work was not always efficacious. It was the middle of October and company A were approaching the height of the busy season. The firm was engaged in the production of two main 'lines', although there were others working their way through the system. Firstly, there was the 'wax' jacket. The wax jacket, apparently 'de rigeur' for farmers and other citizenry associated with the country, was introduced to the market over five years ago. Company A, and many similar concerns in the West Midlands, never really started to produce the jacket in any significant quantity until two years later. It seemed that almost every West Midland clothing manufacturer was assembling this jacket, and the rather predictable outcome was a marked decrease in the price. Nevertheless, company A had managed to produce and sell the jacket consistently over the last three years.

The second jacket in production at this particular point in time was the 'Rockie' jacket, a rather colourful windcheater for children with a 'Rockie' motif. It should have been 'Rocky' (after the film[s]) but the copyright laws prevented it from being so. This garment had been on the market for eighteen months, but company A had only been producing it since September 1990. The demand for the garment was so intense that the proprietor had resorted to 'hiding' the jacket from customers who came to the premises in search of the jacket so that he could supply clients that had existing orders, " We can't make enough of them, everyone wants them ", he claimed. Customers were willing to pay 'cash' for the jackets, some even offered to pay in advance. It was not uncommon for the same customers to delay payment for up to six months after receipt of delivery at other times of the year.

The wax line was a 'steady seller'. Phu could be quite confident that there would be a fairly consistent demand for this type jacket. On the other hand, the 'Rockie' jacket was in great demand now. It was certain to sell in great volumes now and over the next month or so, but beyond that time-scale, it was extremely doubtful that the high level of current sales could have been maintained. This was due to the fact that the 'Rockie' jacket was a relatively high fashion children's garment which was a product area prone to rapid style changes. The wax jacket was more of a 'classic' design.

Given this situation, it would have been 'logical' to step up production of the Rockie jackets while reducing that of the wax coats. The reality, however, was somewhat different. The brothers, who had been assembling wax jackets on and off for the last year or so, would not consider making any other jacket at this time of the year. It was the busy season, work was plentiful and they were by now accustomed to producing the wax jackets. Although they had the expertise and capacity to make the 'Rockie' line, they insisted on remaining with the wax jackets. The brothers realised that it was the 'money' season for them and the firm, they were needed now and, as a consequence, they could expect to have their way, " They've got the production and the quality, and they know it ", claimed Gee. This meant that the Rockie jackets were allocated to less assertive workers on the premises or individual homeworkers. Production of the two jackets was running at 50/50 when it should have been at least 70/30 in favour of the 'Rockie' jackets.

It seemed that the existing pattern of social relations prevented a more 'rational' response to developments in the product market. A number of factors interacted in order to determine this particular outcome. There had been a change in the nature of the product market which, in terms of pure 'rationality', should have been addressed by switching the brothers from the assembly of wax jackets to the then more popular 'Rockie' line. This failed to materialise because Phu and the brothers had come to an agreement which involved the continued provision of particular work. Had it been the 'quiet' season, then it would have been unlikely that the brothers could have held out against sewing the 'Rockie' jackets - instead, the busy season had increased their importance to the firm and consequently, their negotiating power. Had there been kinship ties to buttress the essentially economistic relationship between Phu and the brothers, then Phu may have been able to draw upon that in order to persuade them to produce the 'Rockie' jackets. In this sense, not being of the same caste as Phu afforded the brothers a certain bargaining leverage. Alternatively, had the brothers been regarded as 'slow', Phu could simply have imposed a decision or issued an ultimatum. As it was, a cluster of factors - namely, the product market, the time of the year, the importance of the brothers to the firm and the labour market - acted together to produce an outcome that was not necessarily 'rational', but was regarded as the best way of accommodating the various pressures at that point in time.

Conclusion

The purpose of this chapter was to provide an insight into the nature of shopfloor organisation in typical clothing companies in the West Midlands. On the basis of the case study and survey evidence, it would be unduly simplistic to contend that work is organised in an autocratic fashion. If autocratic work organisations are typified by rational and harshly exploitative systems of production, then the regimes of the case study companies at least fell some way short of this position. The actual system of production concealed a range of conflicting pressures, tensions and constraints that served to exacerbate management's uncertain role in accommodating pressures from the market and negotiations on the shopfloor.

Chapter three demonstrated how the notionally rational policies of casualisation and the use of familial labour in the management of the firm produced contradictory outcomes that highlighted the ambivalent role of management. The same 'bounded rationality' was evident in the organisation of production on the shopfloor. It may have been 'rational' to employ cheap Asian female labour and to fragment work, but it was patently far from simple. The actual process of operationalising this particular system of production involved managing an array of conflicting pressures which resulted in heightened uncertainty, continual negotiations and trade-offs.

Workers ended up in the clothing industry because their options were severely curtailed due to the operation of discrimination in mainstream employment. Few wanted careers as machinists and many, on commencing employment in clothing firms, did not possess any particular skill in this area. But Asian employers here needed labour and did not require workers to negotiate any formal recruitment hurdles. However, this did not necessarily mean that there was no selection procedure. It operated in a more subtle way, usually taking the form of a probationary period masquerading as 'training'. During this period, management and workers alike assessed whether or not they could fit into the pattern of production. Despite the obvious benefits of such informality for management, the consequences of granting workers so much scope to influence recruitment was potentially dysfunctional. Recruits had to slot into a productive system shaped significantly by workers, a practical imperative that did not always accord with the wishes of management.

The actual pattern of production was based on a sectionalised system of work which, in turn, was predicated on specialisation around particular functions. Despite this system, workers were expected to be 'flexible' since they too were not immune from the exigencies of competing in an ever changing market environment. Hence the production system generated a tension between the need for workers to be adaptable and use their creative abilities to solve what were essentially management problems, and encouraging adeptness on a particular function. The rationale for the production system could be construed as autocratic, but, in practice, the situation was rather more diffuse. Management's lack of command over the intricacies of shopfloor organisation, and workers consequent influence over the daily ebb and flow of production accentuated the uncertainties confronting management.

The actual allocation of work further highlighted the complexity of shopfloor organisation. It was not simply a question of matching work available to skill. Rather, the process was mediated by considerations like the product market, the labour market, caste and culture. Company A particularly revealed the subtleties inherent in this process. Work was allocated according to criteria that were not always rational in an economic sense and in a manner that varied according to the particular circumstances of the machinists in question.

What this chapter shows is that the whole process of shopfloor organisation is permeated by an array of considerations that simply do not conform to an autocratic model of organisation. The system of production generates pressures, often contradictory, that have to be managed, and the way in which they are managed requires the active involvement of workers' efforts as well as direction from management. Management, then, were faced with the double-bind of responding to the conflicting pressures emanating from the market while, at the same time, having to negotiate on the shopfloor.

The need to negotiate and the tensions inherent in organising the shopfloor points to the contested nature of the workplace. Yet, despite such uncertainty and informality, management still had to monitor what was happening on the shopfloor in order to establish the terms of the effort bargain. The next chapter examines this process.

5

Fixing the Rate

This chapter explores the nature of the effort bargain in the case study firms. The way in which work was allocated has been discussed, and it was noted that the process involved a number of considerations. The concern here is to examine how management, and indeed workers, put a price on their efforts, how the effort bargain was monitored and how the general pace of work was established.

Discussions of the nature of shopfloor regimes in the clothing industry tend to point to the harshness of management on the one hand and instances of worker resistance on the other. Rainnie, for example, presents management-imposed wage rates, direct supervision and intensive working methods as endemic features of the clothing industry. In studies where workers do appear to react to the severity of management domination, it tends to take the form of conscious, deliberate strategies of resistance. In her account of an American clothing company, Lamphere claimed that

" Workers ... evolved a number of strategies to deal with the piece-rate system, ranging from close track of their own work, protesting at rules that seem unfair and constructing a set of informal rules which reduce 'rate-busting' and spread work more evenly " (1979: 276).

To conceive of workplace relations in the polarised terms of management autocracy and strategies of resistance is far too simplistic. An adequate account would need to illustrate the subtleties inherent within the process of negotiating order on the shopfloor. The study by Cunnison

(1966) of the 'Dee' clothing company goes some way to offering a more nuanced view of relations on the shopfloor. Cunnison showed how individual workers engaged in struggles over the piece-rate, the ways in which workers asserted their independence from management and the extent of mutual dependence between managers and workers.

In common with the Armstrong et al (1981) study, Cunnison highlights the flexibly negotiated nature of the employment relationship in a highly competitive industry. Accordingly, the first section examines how the piece-rate, which was the payment system in the case study firms, was negotiated, since it clearly was a negotiated affair. The case study evidence would seem to suggest that negotiation over the rate is not necessarily as one-dimensional as commonly depicted. The calculation involves an array of factors and workers play an influential role in shaping the often unpredictable outcomes.

After examining the 'cost' of the effort bargain, the manner in which the process was 'policed' will be discussed. This section looks at the nature of supervision. Is it, again, simply a question of management autocracy or is the process more subtle and complex? The case study evidence points to the latter conclusion; it also indicates some differences in the supervisory regime in two of the case study companies which the section aims to explain.

The final section examines issues around the 'pace' of work in these firms. Given the highly competitive nature of the industry, there seems to be an expectation, supported in the literature, that the pace of work in the clothing sector is intense. This assessment is questioned using the case study material, since workers did appear to possess significant influence over the manner and level of effort expended.

Negotiating the Rate

This section examines the processes involved in the calculation of the of the piece-rate in the three case study companies. In the West Midlands clothing industry, unlike much of the industry in general, work study is not much in evidence. In Westwood's study of 'Stitchco' for instance, workers were always 'against the minutes' as were those in Rainnie's investigations. Such examples highlight the severity of the work study system and, like that operational in the Armstrong et al study, point to it being dominated by management with workers having little if any opportunity to influence it.

Evidence from the current investigations, however, illustrate that work study was neither totally pervasive nor dictated entirely by management.

The process of piece-rate negotiation in the three case study companies was a much more complex and contingent affair. The rate was not some immutable imposition prescribed by management, but neither was it necessarily what workers felt was a 'fair' rate for the job. Rather, it was usually the product of individualistic bargains that involved considerations like the time of the year, the type of work, past rates, the availability of external labour, caste and culture. These factors mediated the rate-fixing process and rendered the outcomes unpredictable and not always 'rational'. Moreover, it was often differentially applied within each company and always up for negotiation and re-negotiation, as the following excerpt from the field notes illustrates in relation to company A,

> Darshu, an outworker, returns some completed garments to the factory himself. He then sets about discussing with Phu, the proprietor, a rate for the job. He still has not been paid for previous work done. Together, they discuss how much money is outstanding and what the rate for the 'shell suit' job should be. No records are kept of how much work Darshu has done. The completed shell suits that he has brought with him have not been counted and it is unlikely that they will be. There is no formal accounting system, it is all based on trust.

> When it comes to set the rate, Phu asks Darshu to name his price. Darshu, as usual, refuses to do so. He tells Phu to pay him what he likes. Darshu and Phu have still not agreed a price, but their discussion is interrupted by the arrival of a sub-contractor, Ash, who has also come to talk money. The two will undoubtedly receive different prices for the same garment. Ash is demanding an increase in the price that was previously agreed. Phu will not concede. After much debate, with Ash pointing out the complexity of the garment and Phu claiming that he can get it made for half the price from 'the women outside', a compromise is reached. Agreement is secured on the understanding that Phu will provide Ash with regular work (which Phu cannot really guarantee) and that Ash will give priority to Phu rather than his other customers. Ash points out that his machinists are Muslims, and since this is the fasting season, output will be fairly low for the next month. Phu appears sensitive to this and asks Ash not to push his machinists. It is not clear whether this explanation is genuine or merely a ploy to gain extra time to complete an order.

As well as this differential application of the piece-rate, there appeared to be an expectation that the machinists would use their skill to compensate for the problems in production stemming from market pressures. The following incident from the field notes involving two machinists in company A (who were brothers) demonstrates this point,

> The brothers are complaining about the quality of cutting, " They always cut badly and they don't listen to what we say." They are constantly having to trim and adjust the various elements of the garment that they are trying to sew. In this particular case (a rally jacket), the front flap was too long and the padding that fits between the lining and the outer fabric was incorrectly cut and therefore also had to be altered. These adjustments were time consuming, yet they were not incorporated in the rate that the brothers were receiving for the jacket. In a normal working day (9am to 8pm), they would produce seven of these garments at £3.05 per jacket. They reckoned that if they did not have to correct the cutting mistakes output could increase to ten.

> The faulty cutting was caused by pressure on the cutter to 'get the work out'. He made a judgement regarding what he felt that he could 'get away with'. It was left to the brothers to manipulate the ill-fitting elements of the garment. Nevertheless, Gee claimed that the various parts of the garment being produced by the brothers were being sewn out of sequence, which made it difficult to align the flap and the rest of the jacket accurately. If the flap had been made after the rest of the jacket, there would not have been a problem. The flaps, however, were being sewn first and then attached to the rest of the jacket. This meant that the excessive length of the flaps, which was not disputed by Gee, could not be easily aligned with the rest of the jacket. " They don't think about what they are doing," claimed Gee.

This incident highlights the difficulties of producing a garment to a particular standard under pressure from the market and, indeed, the payment system. The garments in question were not accepted by the customer, the brothers refused to repair them, attributing blame to the cutting. Another machinist was finally paid to repair them.

In company B, the garment would usually be in production for a week before a rate was finally arrived at. The supervisor had an idea of the price based on previous garments, but she would listen to certain machinists whom she 'trusted'. A rate was finally arrived at based on the discussions between the supervisor, the trusted machinists and the firm's partners.

The following incident from the field notes reveals some of the processes involved in this calculation,

> At the moment, the machinists are producing hood jackets, which are regarded as 'difficult' and shell suits, which are considered 'easy'. The machinists are complaining about the complexities of the hood jackets. Output appears to be low and the order is already three weeks late. A production level of in excess of 100 per day was expected compared to an actual level of 60.

> The piece-rate that was initially agreed has not been altered. Some machinists, the finishers in this case, have been harder hit than others. One of the partners says to the machinists " We're making a loss on this order, so you will have to accept it." He promises the finishers more shell suits later on. But have they accepted it ?

> The supervisor has allocated some hood work to a machinist who is currently sewing shell suits. Normally, this machinist can sew at least 80 shell suits a day. However, since she has known that the hood work is waiting for her, she has slowed down. She has had 89 shell suit tops for over two days, yet she has failed to finish them. The supervisor claims that the machinist is hoping that the hoods will be taken by another machinist.

In company C, the managing director, Gel, would find out from the sample machinist, Suneta [his wife] how 'hard' the garment was to manufacture and the extent to which it differed from previous ones. A rate was then set. However, the rate that Suneta and Gel came up with was not necessarily immutable, " The machinists will always moan and try to get more. What we do is come up with a price, say twenty five pence, but then offer the machinists less, say twenty three pence. After they've moaned, we give them twenty five pence " (Suneta).

However, this negotiating strategy was not always successful. In such circumstances, the work was either given out to sub-contractors or the machinists were put on day-rate, "We don't like putting them on day-rate, but if what they ask for is over the limit, and we can't agree, then that is what we have to do." Alternatively, 'the machinists moan and say that they will do it for this price this time but not for the next order. That suits us because the next order will be something different' (Suneta).

In company A, an isolated homeworker received a lower rate than a sub-contractor who was in a position to meet a sudden surge in demand. However, in this case, the homeworker in question will receive work throughout the year since he has known the proprietor for fifteen years and they are of the same caste. There seems to be a tacit agreement that the proprietor will supply work and the homeworker will not sew for anyone else. It is a relationship bound by trust and reinforced by cultural ties. Once the temporary upsurge in demand has subsided the services of the sub-contractor, however, will not necessarily be retained.

In companies B and C, supervisors and management had notional ideas of the rate in mind before the work was actually allocated to the machinists. However, management in both companies were prepared to be swayed by machinist pressure. When there was a dispute, management would use legitimatory arguments about the need to remain competitive, as they did in the Armstrong et al study, particularly during the quiet season or strike informal bargains.

Supervision - Policing the Bargain

The previous section highlights the extent to which the calculation of the piece-rate was a complicated, contested affair often involving a range of considerations, not all of which were necessarily 'rational'. It seemed to be a jointly negotiated process in which the outcomes were far from certain. Yet, despite the fluidity of such arrangements, the outcome still had to be measured in some way. In return for the rate, management required a 'decent' product; the process therefore had to be supervised.

Studies like those of Rainnie and Westwood indicate that this process took the form of close and direct monitoring of the workforce. Managements there were autocratic in the supervision of their workers, and the machinists (in Rainnie's case especially) seemed to be passive against the exercise of such pressure. This section considers the process of supervision in the context of the case study firms.

Supervision and Family Labour

The managements themselves, that is the employers in the case study firms, seemed to be fairly detached from the supervisory process. They were spatially apart from the operatives' shopfloor, actually being situated in a different room from the machinists. The explanation for this physical divide appears to be cultural stemming from gender relationships in Asian society. However, the reasons notwithstanding, the effect of the separation literally was to afford the machinists a certain space which they could play a significant role in shaping, as we saw, for example, in relation to the location of the work stations in the previous chapter. The actual supervisory process will now be examined.

In company B, the person charged with the responsibility of monitoring the shopfloor was a middle-aged English woman, Dor. Dor had been with the company for a number of years and was initially responsible for supervising the English women who had originally worked for the firm as well as the Asian women. Her main functions were to ensure that the machinists were kept supplied with work and 'checking' the quality of the garments. Originally, so Sig of company B claimed,

" Dor had a bit of power, but this petered out. At first it was quite good, she had a bit of authority - you know, Asians were a bit scared of white people. But now, they try and take her for a ride."

Being 'taken for a ride' essentially meant that Dor was engaged on duties other than those of supervision and that the cause of this was the influence of the machinists. This extract from the field notes illustrates the point,

Dor, the supervisor, literally runs from machine to machine as she tries to respond to the calls of the machinists and keep them supplied with work, " Dor, I want top linings and labels " (machinist)

"The cotton on my machine needs changing " (another machinist).

The machinists seem to make continual demands of Dor. She brings the cut work to them, carries the partly completed work to the next machinist in the production chain, replaces broken needles and repairs faulty jackets. Moreover, abuse is often hurled at her, though it is conveyed in Punjabi so she is unable to understand it.

Sig maintained that he actually wanted the supervisor to supervise, meaning that Dor should be monitoring quality rather than 'fetching and carrying'. He felt that Dor was being manipulated because she was 'too weak', "I tell her not to do any work for them but I walk in and she's doing their work. They control her." Dor, however, felt that she did not receive the full support of management when it came to her 'control' function, as she revealed when asked how working here compared with her previous [white] employer,

"There everyone had their positions, there were bosses and workers. We were much more closely watched, more closely controlled. Here it's not like that. You know who the bosses are but they don't act like that."

Despite Dor 'doing their work', the partners were not prepared to take any action for fear of antagonising the machinists. For example, the dirt on the shopfloor sometimes marked the jackets. Whilst Sig, at the packing stage, was applying cleaning fluid to a jacket that had become marked, I asked him why he tolerated such stains on the garment, " If you go in and say there's a mark on your jacket, they'll say there are a lot of marks on your floor," came the reply.

Although Dor was the only 'official' non-family employee vested with the responsibility of monitoring the machinists, the company did have more informal channels, principally through a former machinist, Jeeto. Jeeto started work here fourteen years ago as a machinist and has never worked for anyone else. Being a widow and unable to speak English, she claimed that she felt a certain security in working for the company. Indeed, it was the company to whom she turned when she wanted to buy a house. Management and workers all contributed financially to the deposit that she needed in order to purchase the property that she had wanted.

Jeeto was nominally employed as a packer, but her abilities in this direction were ridiculed by management. As a packer, she was very 'slow' and regarded by everyone there, including the owners, as a joke figure. Why, then, was she kept on ?

"She is not kept on because of her work, but she has her uses, she'll give the workers a bollocking when we ask her to. She's a bit of a snitch " (Sig).

When probed as to what 'a bit of a snitch' meant, Sig said that she 'monitored the workforce and lets us know what the women are saying'. She performed this role as a part of her main function, which was to monitor the quality of the garments. This was a task that she shared with Harry, an Asian man, whose duties consisted primarily of packing and helping out in the cutting area.

The trio of Dor, Harry and Jeeto then were responsible for ensuring that the machinists were kept supplied with work and monitoring the quality of the garments. Dor's quality monitoring function seemed to have been eroded by the demands that the machinists made upon her to keep them supplied with work, move work around the shopfloor, keep lines balanced and repair faulty work. This meant that the 'quality control' function was left increasingly to Jeeto and Harry, who were situated in the cutting room area.

Management in company D regarded quality control as a 'problem'. Each machinist was required to attach an i.d tag on the particular part of the garment that she had assembled. By doing this, it would be possible to trace the identity of the machinist if the garment happened to be faulty. It was ensuring that machinists adhered to this requirement that was proving problematic. Sig claimed that 20 per cent of garments left the machinists' room without i.d tags, and he put this down to intent rather than forgetfulness. According to Sig, the other 'trick' that machinists got up to was to individually put their i.d on all the garments that they produced, but should they make a mistake, remove the i.d on that particular garment. Should they be confronted, they could claim that they were affixing their i.d on their garments, so the garments with i.d missing could not be theirs.

On a particular occasion, a garment was returned because a size 24 lining was attached to a size 34 jacket. Jeeto brought this to the attention of Sig, who duly instructed her to return it to the machinist responsible. Jeeto returned conveying the message "It's your fault" to Sig. Sig believed that the machinist responsible was probably sewing size 24 linings before she started on the 34s. She must have mixed a 24 with the 34s. The machinists were claiming that the person who allocated the work, either Sig or Dor, must have mistakenly put a 24 with the 34s. Nevertheless, Sig argued that they should think about what they are doing, and that attaching a 24 lining to 34 jacket was obviously indicative of the fact someone that was not thinking, " They should quality control their own garments." The faulty garment was repaired by Dor.

On another occasion, the strips on a garment were put in incorrectly. They were not tucked in properly "We told them to put them in this way, the stupid twats have put it in wrong "(Sig). I asked if it would have taken longer to put them in the way that he had requested. " Yes" Sig replied. In this case the machinist (an outworker) was not reprimanded or asked to rectify the error because she was the wife of one of the partners. Her husband informed her of the error and asked her to produce the rest in the required fashion.

It might be useful to attempt an explanation of such events by contrasting it with the situation in company C, where the shopfloor appeared much 'quieter' than in company B. The two supervisors in company C, both of whom were the wives of men who managed the firm, were also responsible for ensuring that the machinists were kept supplied with work and quality control. In their quality control duties, they were supported by a packing section of four people which was headed by another family member. The supervisors spent little time 'fetching and carrying', neither did they move around the shopfloor in the near frantic way that Dor did in company B. Moreover, they did not repair faulty garments.

In this company too each machinist had to affix her i.d on the particular part of the garment that she had sewn. However, rectifying mistakes was not regarded as a problem for two reasons. Firstly, there were comparatively few mistakes. Secondly, each machinist did attach her i.d to her work, and when a mistake was made, it was easy to trace and not really disputed by the machinist or regarded as problematic by management. Why then was the supervisory process seemingly so much more contested in company B than it was in company C and why was mistake rectification a particular problem in B and not in C ?

One significant factor in explaining the differing degrees to which the supervisory process was contested appeared to be the pervasiveness of family personnel. It seemed that being a family member conferred a certain legitimacy in the workplace that was rarely questioned. In company B, there was no family member on the shopfloor; it was 'policed' solely by a non-family employee who struggled to discharge the burden of the often contradictory responsibilities placed on her - keeping the line flowing, yet monitoring quality, for example. In her 'control' function, she received little support from management who simply wanted to 'get the pieces out' and were wary of taking any action that would antagonise the machinists. Company C, in contrast, had a significant family presence on the shopfloor, especially in the quality control areas.

Being a family member then appeared to be important in accounting for the authority enjoyed by supervisors in company C. Non-family members seemed to have a more difficult time as Dor's experience indicated. Harry, too, confirmed this in relation to his own role. When the three partners had to go out Harry was often expected to 'keep an eye on the women', but, he contended,

> "I can't say anything to them, they'll tell me to fuck off. Not only that they'll give me a load of shit. They spread rumours about me being a boss's lackey." This being the case, Harry does not 'tell them off' even though Sig ostensibly puts him in charge, "I tried to do it before but all they say is 'who the hell are you'" said Harry in apparent despair.

The legitimacy of non-family members in a supervisory role, formal or informal, was clearly not accepted by workers in company B despite the fact that, as in Dor's case, their technical competence was often far in excess of that of family members. There was a similar situation in company A that was highlighted in an incident involving Gee and the packers.

On a particular occasion Phu, the proprietor, was away. In his absence, he had asked Gee to ensure that an urgent order which was currently being processed was checked and packed so that it would be ready for delivery. Gee was contemptuous of the three packers' efforts ostensibly because they were 'lazy',

" It's taken those bastards five minutes to pack one jacket. I've told them to check and pack the jackets but all they say is 'wait a minute, wait a minute'. I was here 'till 9 pm last night packing jackets; why am I the only one who works hard? "

It was clear that despite Gee's instructions and his position within the firm, his authority was not unquestioned. The packers would not accept a 'bollocking' from Gee in the passive way that they would from Phu or any other member of the family. An exchange followed between Gee and Bal, a packer:

Gee " How come it takes you so long to check the jackets."

Bal " We've been busy, can't you see."

Gee " I've been watching you, you've done fuck all for the last ten minutes. If you're not going to do the jackets, take these rolls (of material) upstairs."

Bal " I'll take them up when I'm ready."

Gee " You'll find out when Phu comes back."

Bal " We'll see."

A few minutes later, Bas (son of Phu) walked on to the shopfloor and asked Bal to check the jackets. Bal proceeded with the task straight away.

Bal (to me)

"We've finished the work boss, what shall we do next? "In mocking tones he continues " Will the other gaffer (meaning Gee) know?"

Hence, the extent of family involvement on the shopfloor would seem to be an important factor in explaining differences in shopfloor behaviour. However, an equally significant consideration, with particular explanatory importance for the mistake rectification issue, was the nature of the payment system.

Role of Payment System

In both companies B and C, workers were usually paid on piece-rate. In company B, this was a seemingly permanent feature, but in company C, it was not uncommon for machinists to be put on day-rate when they switched jobs. Consequently, when machinists in company B had to perform work other than their specialist function, they were still paid on piece-rate, while workers in company C could expect the financial burden of the job switch to be alleviated, to some degree at least, by payment on a day-rate basis. A number of machinists in company B admitted that they tended to make more mistakes whilst engaged on work other than their specialism and it would seem that this was due to their attempts to come to terms with the payment system.

Making 'mistakes' was not part of a deliberate strategy by workers against the nature of the payment system. These mistakes were not intentional and machinists did not somehow view them as conscious acts of resistance. Rather, they were an outcome made more likely by the nature of a particular payment system. Workers tried to escape detection in an attempt to maintain a degree of stability in their level of earnings. Coping with rapid style changes without the cushion of day-rate was difficult enough without having to incur the cost of work already done.

Contesting mistake rectification was not the only product of the payment system. Machinists, in some instances, attempted to increase their supply of 'easy' work by only partially completing their allotted work, and then asking for more work. On a particular occasion in company B, it was coming to the end of an order and a new line was being introduced. Gurd, a machinist had asked for more work despite the fact that she had 21 pieces hidden in her work box. These 21 pieces had, in fact, been completed, but Gurd had wanted to pass them on to her friend down the line rather than let Dor allocate the work. Dor discovered the work and passed it on to another machinist.

Another effect was that workers appeared to guard closely their particular specialism. For instance, on one occasion, four finishers had been sewing 'difficult' jackets at a rate of 60 per day (15 each). Two pocket hands, who had finished their quota of pocket work, were asked to move on to finishing, and almost immediately, production of this particular jacket had gone up to 150 per day. Why ? Sig attributed this to 'jealousy of the finishers'. Apparently, they did not want anyone else to do their work, so they worked faster. Now the average rate per individual was 25 rather than 15. This increase could not be explained by the machinists becoming familiar with the garments since the pocket hands had not finished this garment before and they had no problem in reaching 25 pieces per day. Dor agreed with Sig's interpretation, claiming that the machinists jealously guarded their own jobs.

Referring to the incident, Dor contended that the four original finishers responded to the arrival of the pocket hands on 'their work' by 'working harder', " They don't want anyone else to do their jobs. There seems to be a conspiracy." She claimed "that they race against each other when someone new comes on the job".

The problem of 'jealousy' was also evident when machinists took work home. There were two machinists in company B who regularly took work home after their stint at the factory. Sig claimed that this often caused resentment amongst the rest of the machinists "because they're jealous". According to Sig, this had two effects. Firstly, the women complained that there was not enough work for the machinists on site. Sig claimed that this was unfounded because the machinists were always kept well supplied; he attributed this complaint once again to 'jealousy'. Secondly, to avoid this 'jealousy', work that was to be taken home was often distributed covertly to the machinists in question away from the gaze of other operatives.

These scenarios, which management put down to 'jealousy', were again outcomes made more likely by management operating the payment system in a particular way rather than a coherent, deliberate strategy of worker resistance. It was 'rational' for workers to try to hang on to work that they had become adept at performing for as long as they could. The next line could be 'difficult' or 'easy', no one really knew until it was in production. Management might decide to get the next order assembled by sub-contractors or homeworkers, it might be a large order or it could be another short run. There was no compensation for tackling these uncertainties. It is against this background of imponderables that attempts by machinists to preserve 'their work' must be viewed.

The actions of the machinists towards this end were opportunistic rather than strategic. An illustration of this point was related by Sig in an incident involving a machinist and the introduction of a new line, denim jackets. For the first week on this product, the machinist was earning £40 compared with her normal weekly wage of £70. She kept on complaining that the jacket was too difficult and that the rate should be increased. Sig accepted her contentions. In the following week, her wages rose to £200 per week, and this continued for the next month. How did Sig react? "What can you do. She did us, fair do's".

The type of activity outlined above in relation to company B was an attempt by workers to adjust the terms of the effort bargain. Both Roy

(1954) and Lupton (1963) in their studies demonstrated the various ways in which workers attempted to alter the effort bargain. Lupton, for example, in his study of the 'Jay Engineering Company', analysed a range of 'fiddles' used by workers to control their earnings. One such 'fiddle' was not to book batches of completed work in order to even out earnings over a period of time. It was Lupton's contention that such 'fiddles' were rational and represented an attempt by workers to secure a stable relationship between work and effort.

In the case of company B, workers 'making mistakes', partially completing work, speeding-up on certain jobs and taking work home was similarly rational. It was the means by which machinists endeavoured to exercise an element of control over the level of their earnings.

On the basis of the prevalence of these kinds of practices, Sig claimed that 'they [the machinists] cheat, lie and deceive' and maintained that there was a lack of 'honesty' in the workplace. Yet, at the same time, there was also a considerable amount of trust placed in workers, as exemplified by the way in which machinists' output was recorded. It was essentially a four stage process:

1. The person doing the cutting would record how many pieces had been cut and which batch they belonged to in the cutting book.
2. Each machinist made a note of how many pieces she had sewn per day.
3. One of the machinists, Shardra, recorded each machinist's output on a daily basis. She did this by asking individual machinists, not by counting the number of pieces made.
4. At the end of the week, Shardra would present the records, with the wages calculated, to the partners. The partners then would hand over the wage packets to Shardra who duly conveyed them to the machinists.

This process was undoubtedly cheap, as far as management were concerned at any rate, since Shardra was only paid an additional £5 for her efforts. But the essential point is the considerable degree of trust that was placed in machinists by recording output in this way. There were, potentially, a number of 'plausible' reasons why the quantity calculated by Shardra need not have tallied with the amount of work cut by management. For example, the cutters could have incorrectly counted the number of lays, they could have tied the bundles of work improperly (putting more in one batch and less in another), labels could have been mixed up and so on. Yet, Sig claimed that it was very rare that Shardra had to cross reference her figures with the records in the cutting room, " We trust the women to tell us how much they make."

Not only could they be 'trusted' to provide to accurate honest records of their output, they could be relied on to come in at weekends and holidays should they be required to do so. Part of this fieldwork was conducted over the Bank Holiday period when the machinists came in as usual. They did not receive any additional payments; they merely responded to a request from management.

To a certain extent, this 'honesty' and 'reliability' can be explained by the economic reality of this particular employment relationship. As mentioned earlier, many machinists here worked 'off the books' or declared only a portion of their earnings. During the holiday periods, workers who actually took their leave entitlements were not paid what they would have earned on piece-rate. Rather, they were paid according to their declared income. Hence a worker earning £100 per week, but only declaring £40, would only be paid £40 if she were to take a week's holiday. It was not uncommon for management to ask workers who wanted to go on holiday to 'take a week sick' in order to make up the shortfall. Hence machinists who work during the holidays may do so because they are not in a position to suffer the financial burden of not earning their piece-rate wages.

'Reliability' therefore was often based on economic necessity, but in highlighting this point, factors like 'loyalty' should not be discounted. In all three case study companies, workers seemed to show a particular loyalty to the respective firms. Each company had employees with over ten years' service who seemed to have a certain allegiance to the firm in question despite the availability of similar work in similar companies. Certain machinists in company B lived over five miles away, which was a relatively long distance for workers of this kind to travel. For these workers to partake in practices like systematically distorting output figures would have meant that the 'comfortable' working relationships that had been developed would have been jeopardised and they would further face the prospect of starting again in an unfamiliar set-up not knowing where they would fit in the production process. Hence it seemed that deliberately fiddling output levels was seen as illegitimate by workers and management alike, while attempts to come to terms with job switches were regarded as legitimate, although management saw this as problematic.

The discussion so far has revealed the contested nature of the rate-fixing and supervisory processes. Yet, despite these negotiations, there seemed to be an informal understanding over the terms of the effort bargain. Wages, as the survey evidence indicated, were not particularly good in these companies and the industry in general, a fact that seemed to be acknowledged by most machinists. The machinists therefore were operating in a context that was heavily constricted. Moreover, since many of them were, through racism, excluded from the more privileged sections of the labour market, their options were limited. However, what they did have was significant discretion over was their level of effort and the manner in which work was performed. It is to this influence over the pace of work that we now turn.

Work Pace

Informality and Traditionalism

Machinists in all three companies talked quite freely to their colleagues, they had breaks when they wanted and in many cases, came and went when they pleased. In company B, two machinists collected their children at 11.55am, returned ten minutes later and often fed them on the premises. A number of machinists in this factory claimed that a major reason for starting work here was due to the fact that the premises were close to the local school, and that the boss did not mind them taking time off should the need arise. Another machinist in this factory regularly left at 11.55am in order to serve at the newsagent's that her family owned. She returned at 1pm but left again at 3.25pm, which was apparently the start of another busy period in the newsagent. She finally returned at 4pm. Around half of the machinists went home for lunch taking a full hour, while the rest remained at their work-stations and took only fifteen minutes. The length of these breaks was entirely in the hands of the machinists.

Machinists seemed to enjoy considerable discretion over the actual ways in which they worked. In company B, Dor, a trained instructor, claimed that the methods used by machinists in their individual operations were 'inefficient'. Each machinist was responsible for a particular operation, for example, pockets, linings, finishing and so on. According to Dor, the 'efficient' way to carry out the task would have been to sew an item of the part of the garment that they were engaged upon and then proceed to the next one. Hence the pocket hand, for instance, would sew one pocket before moving on to the next one. This pocket could then be transferred to the next stage of production. What actually happened was that the pocket hand would sew a particular part of the pocket at a time. The next machinist would have to wait until the pocket hand had completed the various stages of the entire batch of pockets before she could start her job. The work was thus received en bloc rather than sequentially, thus leading to imbalances in the production flow. Below are examples of the 'efficient' method and the actual method.

Linings

Efficient

1.	Join shoulders	}	Garment should not be handled more than three
2.	Put sleeves in	}	times.
3.	Join side seams	}	

Actual

1.	Join all shoulders	}	Garment handled five times
2.	Stop to cut cottons off	}	
3.	Put all sleeves in	}	
4.	Stop to cut cottons off	}	
5.	Join parts	}	(The joiners perform their function in a similar way)

Pockets

Efficient

1.	Make a pair of flaps	}	This should be done without
2.	Put pocket linings on	}	putting the garment down.
3.	Cut it to put flap on	}	
4.	Stitch around pocket	}	

Actual

1.	Make all flaps	}	Garment is put down four times.
2.	Put all the linings on	}	
3.	Cut it and stitch around pockets	}	

Trousers

Efficient
1. Put stripes in   } Front
2. Join front seam/ put
   pockets on
3. Join middle and
   back/ put other pocket
   in   } Back
4. Join back and front
   and put elastic in   }

Actual
1. Make all stripes for all trousers
2. Attach stripes to trousers
3. Join the front seams Eight stages
4. Join all the back seams
5. Put the pockets on
6. Join all the side seams
7. Put elastic in
8. Join the middle

Why did they work in this manner? Dor claimed that it was due to them 'always doing it that way'. She did try to change the methods but the machinists would not accept new ways of working. Although the result was often bottlenecks in production, 'their way', in fact, was quicker for them as individual machinists. This seemed to be the main reason why they would not change. Sig was asked why he tolerated this method of production. He said that he was not really bothered because 'we get our pieces out at the price that we want them'. His particular way of addressing the bottleneck was to adjust his cutting schedules, overlapping orders where necessary and holding back work when required.

On a particular occasion, the machinists were having problems in aligning a top stitch on a particular jacket in the required way. They could not sew it in a straight line. Sig sought technical help and was duly advised that the problem could be easily resolved by using a special machine foot. The machinists claimed that they could not use the machine foot despite the fact that Sig, who was not a machinist, demonstrated the process to them, " It was a doddle ", he claimed. The machinists' reluctance to operate the machine foot did not stem from a lack of ability. Rather, they were unwilling to adopt the particular method of working required if the machine foot was to be utilised. By the end of the day, they had reverted back to the former practice.

Five years ago, Sig brought a pocket welting machine for £12,500. This was a considerable sum at the time given the fact that an ordinary industrial sewing machine costs around £400. Making pockets was one of the most complex machining operations; this machine would make it much easier and cheaper,

" It deskilled the job. Instead of paying an experienced machinist 40 pence a pocket, we can get someone in off the street and pay them half the amount " claimed Sig.

The machinists, however, contended that they could make the pockets quicker on the old machines and were not prepared to either work the new machine or move to other operations. The machine now lies unused in a corner of the machinists' room. Sig did not force the issue because he was getting his 'pieces out'. Making a general comment about the machinists, Sig claimed that " It's like the old unions, restrictive practices. That's what they do."

Machinists in company C also seemed resistant to any attempt by management to alter their ways of working. Seven years ago, Gel brought in some consultants because he was concerned about the 'low' level of production. The consultants recommended the implementation of a work study system, which entailed timing individual machinists and altering their working methods. When Gel attempted to implement the recommendations, the machinists threatened to walk out, " They weren't having any of it. They said if you want us to work like that, we're going." The plans were hastily abandoned because "we needed the machinists". According to Gel, work study would only be successful "if you have machinists of different cultures. Our women won't have it".

Machinists commenting on this particular event were insistent that they were not going to change. These were two typical reactions,

"We weren't worried about them [the consultants]. We came to work and just carried on in our own way."

" It doesn't matter if they say we're too fast or too slow, we work at our own pace whether on day-work or piece-work."

The way in which machinists worked in the case study companies was 'locally rational' in the sense that workers felt that they could expedite their tasks more rapidly in this manner. It was sensible for them to work in this way. However, in terms of the overall or total productive system, the adoption of this method rather than the sequential way of working was not efficient or rational because it resulted in bottlenecks and imbalances in the flow of production. It was, indeed, a management problem which was not addressed because the prevailing social relations of production.

In making this point, it is possible to draw on Lazonick's (1981) study of the British cotton industry in the nineteenth century. Lazonick argues that the failure of the British cotton industry to adapt its production processes on the basis of advanced technologies in the first half of this century was due to the structure of industrial organisation. Britain lagged significantly behind its competitors in the adoption of new cotton manufacturing processes.

Employers, mainly in Lancashire, blamed their inability to compete with the cotton industries of Western Europe and the United States on the shortage of labour, but the real issue was the industry's failure to invest in the capital equipment that would have allowed it to offer the wages and conditions required to attract an adequate supply of labour. The British cotton industry failed to restructure its industrial organisation to meet the increased competition of the twentieth century because any serious attempt to have done so would have had profound implications for workers, managers and the well-established organisation of work. Few managers had the ability or incentive to participate in the transformation of the industry. It seemed that the social relations of production thwarted the emergence of a more rational global system of production.

As in the Lazonick study, both management and workers in the current study were locked into a particular pattern of production. Despite its apparent simplicity, irrationality and eccentricity, the system of production in place in many West Midlands clothing firms had enabled them to survive in a highly competitive market environment. Such firms may not have been spectacularly successful, but they were still in existence. This survival was due to the flexibility of their organisation and their ability to come to terms with the vagaries of the market. Despite the 'rigidities' on the shopfloor, management were still largely able to 'get the pieces out', although perhaps not with the precision and certainty that they would have liked. For example, Gel of company C often despaired at the sheer unpredictability of the machinists and the problems that it caused in meeting delivery schedules. However, when deadlines were looming, it was not uncommon for machinists to mobilise their efforts towards despatching the order, 'As soon as you approach a delivery date and you think it's not going to be met, everyone drops everything else and tries to get it out', claimed Gel.

This 'mad dash' as it was described by Gel, was a regular occurrence and expensive too since it often entailed paying machinists moving from less urgent work on a day-rate basis. However, given the configuration of workplace relations and the constraints of the market, it was regarded, often reluctantly, as the only way of operating.

Of course, it was not the only way of operating. There were more 'rational' forms of organisation predicated on new technology, a multi-skilled workforce, planned production and a more sophisticated management. However, there was no institutional mechanism of moving from the locally rational system of production to a globally rational one. To have attempted such a leap would have necessitated fundamental changes in work organisation involving management as well as workers.

Moreover, the introduction of new technology would have required considerable sums of investment which typical clothing firms in the West Midlands could ill afford and saw no need of given their reliance on cheap labour (Lloyd, 1989). Hence despite the constant exhortations to move 'up-market' (Totterdill and Zeitlin, 1989) and the supposed benefits of a 'flexible specialisation' scenario (Piore and Sabel, 1984), it seemed that employers in the West Midlands clothing industry, like those in Lazonick's study, had neither the ability nor incentive to undertake the initiatives required to secure a more globally rational system of production.

Management Tolerance

The flexibility within the productive system may have facilitated the survival of West Midlands clothing firms, but it also occasioned considerable tension and uncertainty. Given the extremely competitive nature of the market, why did management tolerate this state of affairs? Before tackling this question directly, the issue of discipline should be addressed, since it seems that disciplinary procedures were largely absent. Employers interviewed in the survey stage of the study did not perceive discipline to be a problem. This was probably due to the 'training' period. If workers were not suitable, or if they did not like the work, then employment would be terminated. The majority of employees left because of pregnancy or to find better work; few were sacked.

Despite the numerous examples of worker assertiveness in the case study companies, none of the employers invoked any disciplinary measures. On a particular occasion in company B, one of the machinists had completed her batch of linings. Sig, through Dor, asked her to perform a different operation. The machinist refused and went home. No action was taken on her return the following day. On another occasion in the same company, the machinists had inserted the wrong colour collar on the garments. Sig contended that it was Dor's fault because, as the supervisor, it was her job to check the quality. The mistake cost £400 to rectify since the machinists had to be paid on a day-rate basis to correct the order. No action was taken against Dor. Why did management put up with this state of affairs ?

Edwards (1988) reviews a number of reasons why management might do so. Management may want to give workers some interest in their job. Allowing discretion could help to reduce more costly adaptation like fiddling or absenteeism. They might sustain a system of low pay or arbitrary power or, as Burawoy contends, 'game playing' could work in management's interests. In the context of this study, however, two factors seemed particularly germane in serving as constraints upon managerial prerogative, namely the labour market and ethnicity.

The previous chapter noted that many employers complained of a 'labour shortage'. This shortage, however, was a shortage of cheap immigrant labour. Nevertheless, management appeared to believe that it was a significant constraint. On a number of occasions, Sig of company B made the point that he did not 'get rid' of particular machinists because of the 'labour shortage', meaning a dearth of Asian women prepared to accept low wages.

Company C provides an even more potent example. Two years previously, the firm faced a serious downturn in demand. The machinists were not receiving enough work to earn anything like a decent wage. In Hoel's study, management sacked or laid off workers when there was any sign of recession (1982: 85). In company C, the workers were all put on day-rate, and this state of affairs lasted for over a year. Management claimed that the reason for holding on to the machinists was the difficulty of recruiting skilled labour.

The perpetual seasonal uncertainty stemming from rapid style changes, the need to turn round orders quickly and the general unpredictability of the market seemed to give workers a certain power - a 'seasonal' power. The cyclical nature of the market did seem to enhance machinists' bargaining resources. However, this did not necessarily mean that workers were inevitably 'disempowered' during the 'quieter' times of the year. Employers in the three case study companies, and indeed those taking part in the survey, claimed that they always kept their machinists 'busy'. This was not a reference to the pace or intensity of work. Rather, it meant that they kept their machinists supplied with enough work so that they could earn a 'decent' wage on piece-rate. This appeared to be almost independent of the state of their order books. It seemed that employers dare not let machinists go for fear of not being able to compete in the 'busy' season.

The state of the labour market then was regarded as an important restraint upon management, allowing workers leeway that they may not have had in other circumstances. However, despite the significance that employers in the current study accorded to the state of the labour market in shaping their behaviour towards workers, it is important to guard against the notion of deterministic explanations of work organisation.

Studies investigating the link between the labour market and the firm (Brown, 1973; Nolan and Brown, 1983) have tended to conclude that there is no direct link between the state of the labour market and employment structure within the firm. For example, in their study of 25 engineering firms in the West Midlands over a five year period Nolan and Brown (1983) found that employers exercised a considerable degree of discretion in the wage-setting process. Rubery (1988), reviewing a range of empirical studies, observed that there was 'no evidence to support deterministic explanations of work organisation, whether technological or market based' (p263).

The analysis of the labour market, then, should not be abstracted from issues within the labour process. But, at the same time, the organisation of labour within firms needs to be informed by the competitive position of firm within the industry. Taken together, it is the social relations of production and the mediated impact of 'external' factors that will 'ultimately shape and underpin the existing structure of employment, the job opportunities available to particular groups within the labour market, and the path and development of industrial relations in particular companies' (Nolan, 1983: 309).

In the light of these points the pattern of workplace relations in the current study cannot be seen as a function of the labour market. The dynamics of the shopfloor, the processes involves in negotiation and accommodation and the general organisation of work were the product of a number of interacting factors that had their own particular dynamics. It is doubtful whether developments in the labour market would have radically altered relations on the shopfloor. As in the case of competition discussed in chapter one, the labour market may have contributed to the pattern of workplace relations, but its impact too had to be mediated.

Moreover, it was not the labour market per se, it was a particular kind of labour, namely cheap Asian female labour. Many studies of ethnic enterprise (Wallman, 1979: Werbner, 1984) have tended to highlight the extent to which ethnicity has been a 'resource'. Hence, to claim that ethnicity does, in certain circumstances, act as a constraint upon management goes against the grain of the general image of Asian workers. The next chapter examines the multi-faceted nature of ethnicity and offers a more rounded view of the concept.

Conclusion

This chapter has explored the issues around the negotiation of the effort bargain in the three case study firms. What the evidence seems to show is that it would be unduly simplistic to characterise the effort bargaining process as management autocracy. The whole process was permeated by an often disparate amalgam of variables which rendered the outcomes of such negotiations unpredictable. The only area that was apparently immune from negotiation was the actual booking of work. Workers would not deliberately manipulate the recording of work and management, in turn, were quite prepared to entrust this task to workers. However, this apart, given the tensions inherent in establishing the terms of the effort bargain, neither autocracy nor resistance was an accurate assessment of the nature of work relations.

In negotiations around the actual piece-rate, management and workers struck informal bargains or came to an understanding based on considerations like the particular time of the season, the availability of external labour, the labour market, caste and culture. Such outcomes were not predicated on calculations deriving from sophisticated work study systems, nor was it simply a case of 'management intuition' as it appeared to be in Hoel's study of apparently similar companies. Management's grip over the rate-fixing process was clearly not as unrelenting as it was in the studies by Westood and Rainnie.

'Policing' the rate was again more complicated than management simply bearing down on workers and highlighted the tensions inherent in the process of rate-fixing. Indeed, it was possible to discern differences between workplaces stemming from the negotiation of the piece-rate. Workers were not passive in the face of authoritarian managements; they would endeavour to alter the terms of the effort bargain if they felt that they were not 'fairly' rewarded. In company B, where this was evidently a 'problem', these endeavours took the form of 'mistakes', the stockpiling of work and 'modifying' the role of the supervisor. Such actions illustrated the contested nature of the shopfloor, but cannot be regarded as deliberate strategies of resistance. Rather, they were opportunistic and pragmatic actions by workers attempting to secure a degree of stability over their earnings.

The fluidity of the piece-rate negotiations and the supervisory process was equally apparent in issues surrounding the pace of work. Workers accepted that they were in a highly competitive and low paying industry; they appreciated the inevitability of job switching and they realised that discrimination severely constrained their employment opportunities. In other words, machinists were aware of the straitened context in which bargaining took place. However, the quid pro quo appeared to be discretion over the manner and level of effort expended, and any attempt by management to alter this informal agreement was tackled by means ranging from outright resistance to 'trickery' in the form of 'mistakes,' and so on. Machinists had established their own ways of working which made sense to them but were not efficient in terms of the overall productive system. Management, however, did not have the resolve, initiative or incentive to undertake the changes required to move to a more rational total system of production. The result was almost continual uncertainty, although management appeared to tolerate the situation as long as they got their orders out.

Employers further tolerated the autonomy of their workers because of the apparent 'labour shortage', or at least that is what they claimed. Although it was becoming increasingly difficult to recruit 'skilled' machinists, the character of workplace relations cannot be explained by the state of the labour market. Rather, traditions at the workplace develop over time and have their own particular logics and dynamics. Any effect that the labour market might have will be mediated by these traditions. Moreover, in the context of the current study, it is not any kind of labour - the labour in question is cheap Asian female labour. This is the discussed in the next chapter.

The highly informal, fluid and contested nature of negotiations around the rate-fixing process presented here is at variance with the accounts of managerial domination offered by Armstrong et al, Westwood and Rainnie in their studies. In the light of these findings, it is probably the case that the clothing industry in general is less autocratic than some, certainly Rainnie, suggest. However, it would be premature to conclude that the degree of informality inherent within the negotiation of the rate is the same throughout the clothing sector. Clearly there are obvious differences, not least being the size of the firms involved.

The bureaucratic and autocratic means of establishing the rate in the studies by Edwards and Scullion (1982), Westwood and even Rainnie illustrated the tendency towards more rational forms of organisation as firm size increased. This, however, does not mean that room for negotiation is eliminated - rather, the scope for informality and flexibility is progressively organised out in larger firms. It is arguably necessary for larger firms to utilise sophisticated forms of work study in order to secure the necessary uniformity and control over the productive process required to compete in a highly competitive market environment.

Employers in West Midlands clothing firms were also operating in hostile markets, but the particular constraints that they were working under meant that they were reliant to a large extent on the efforts of their workers. The informality of the social relations of production may not have been 'rational', but it was flexible and the firms were still in existence. These points are developed and located in a more general context in the concluding chapter. The point to emphasise is that informality, despite its uncertainties, appeared to have worked for manufacturers in the West Midlands clothing sector.

6

Ethnicity at the Workplace

This chapter explores the significance of 'ethnicity' in the West Midlands clothing sector. It is not about comparing what is peculiarly Asian with that which is distinctively British. The experience of white workers and employers is not set alongside that of their black counterparts. Rather, the discussion will demonstrate the extent to which ethnicity is a significant factor in shaping outcomes on the shopfloor.

Following Phizacklea, I will take ethnicity to be 'the recognition and maintenance of cultural difference' (1990: 5). In adopting this simple definition, it is not intended that the discussion will be preoccupied with examining the internal characteristics of a particular ethnic minority group. The purpose here is not to ruminate on the idiosyncrasies, subtleties and specificities of Asian culture in abstract. Although it is important to recognise the significance of particular features of Asian culture, ethnicity can only be properly understood in relation to the wider context in which it operates. Most importantly, ethnicity needs to be considered against a background of racism and economic decline in British society. The first of three sections in this chapter assesses the context of structured racism in which ethnic minority firms find themselves.

There is continuing evidence of the prevalence of racism and racial discrimination in British society (Brown, 1984). An appreciation of ethnicity, therefore, needs to be sensitive to this context. However, in making this point, it does not follow that minority groups are passive in the midst of the oppressive forces that face them. They draw upon their own resources in a bid to overcome these constraints. Access to 'family' and community labour has been widely regarded as perhaps the most important of these resources in establishing small labour-intensive businesses. The second section critically examines the notion of 'family' labour, since it is clear that access to family labour as a resource usually means access to cheap female labour. The viability of ethnic enterprise is predicated on the labour of minority women, a point which the current study emphasises again in this section. Minority women work for minority men, not alongside them. This is facilitated by the patriarchal and familial ideologies of particular groups. Within the context of the present study, the minority women in question were Punjabi Sikhs in companies B and C. Company A did not employ any women machinists on the shopfloor for reasons explained in chapter two - the few operatives that did sew on the premises were male Sikhs and of various castes.

The 'values' of minority groups combine with the impact of racist and sexist practices in the labour market and immigration legislation to reinforce women's subordinate position in ethnic enterprise. However, minority women do not necessarily accept these constraining forces in quiescent fashion. They too call upon their own, culturally specific, resources, and in doing so are able to influence their working environment. Minority women can 'use' their culture to make space for themselves on the shopfloor. The final section presents material from the case study companies which illustrates ways in which women workers actively deploy the culture that is so often perceived to oppress them.

In outlining ethnicity in this particular way, two points should be evident. Firstly, ethnicity is inextricably linked with gender, family and racism; and secondly, it is a fluid concept capable of working for women as well as men. The discussion begins with an assessment of the context of racism.

The Context of Racism

The ways in which racism inhibits Asian entrepreneurs and labour needs to be set out in order to grasp the significance of ethnicity. Jones's (1992) research on ethnic enterprise concentrates primarily on Asian involvement in retailing, but his three-fold account of ethnic minority small businesses provides a useful means of understanding the constraints upon Asian entrepreneurs in the West Midlands clothing sector. The first proposition is that small business itself in relation to large enterprise is structurally disadvantaged in that large firms continue to dominate the economy. Secondly, Asian involvement in small business can only be understood in relation to a racially biased job market which severely limits their employment opportunities. Thirdly, Asian entrepreneurs are subject to a further set of constraints which confine them to the least well rewarded sectors of production and exchange. These points will now be considered in more detail.

Large Firm - Small Firm

Jones's explanation of the survival of the small firm is not too dissimilar from Rainnie's analysis. Both stress the dominance/dependence relationship between large and small capital. Small firms still exist although they are clearly subordinate to large capital which has monopoly control over the business resources upon which petty production depends. Consequently, petty capital's continued survival is due, in large part, to its capacity to provide service to large capital. With regard to petty retailing, this is commonly provided by small, usually Asian, retailers operating on the peripheral parts of the consumer market that monopoly retailing refuses to reach on account of low returns and unacceptable margins. In Rainnie's presentation of the garment industry, large and powerful retailers like Marks and Spencer were in a position where they could virtually control the small clothing manufacturers that supplied them. Retailers could squeeze the margins of dependent manufacturers in recessionary times and use them to ride out periods of uncertainty.

In the context of the West Midlands clothing industry, the large firm/ small firm divide was not perhaps as great as that identified by Jones and Rainnie, but there was still evidence of a dependent relationship. The few firms supplying retailers directly were subject to quite stringent controls. Manufacturers supplying retailers through agents, like companies B and C, were often used to 'top-up' orders that were originally placed elsewhere. The relationship between Cut, Make and Trim firms and larger manufacturers was also characterised by a high degree of risk and uncertainty.

Replacement Labour

The predominance of ethnic minorities in sectors like clothing and retailing leads to Jones's second point concerning racism in the labour market,

" Just as Asian workers have acted as replacement labour in many low wage industries with undesirable working conditions, so in the guise of petty capitalists they now bear the brunt of retailing in various market niches progressively abandoned by the white trader" (1992: 11).

The same could undoubtedly be said of the clothing sector in the West Midlands.

The Asian-dominated West Midlands clothing sector was a comparatively recent phenomenon. Before the 1970s, clothing was not a particularly significant industry in the region, and what little that there was tended to be controlled by large firms manufacturing traditional lines such as men's outerwear (Hayden, 1992). The economic onslaught of the recession, however, precipitated the closure or relocation of these predominantly white firms. It also created the high levels of unemployment among the large Asian community in the area, further restricting their opportunities within mainstream employment. These were the conditions that gave rise to the West Midlands clothing sector.

It was noted in chapter three that the comparatively high level of Asian involvement in the West Midlands clothing industry was a product of racism rather than any particular cultural predisposition towards entrepreneurship. Respondents interviewed in the survey stage of the study stressed that to become self-employed was the only way that they could hope to earn a decent living. The choice lay between the drudgery of poorly rewarded factory work or the possibility of achieving something better through enterprise. It was clear that racism in the wider labour market prevented advancement from being achieved through mainstream employment, a point that was equally relevant to minority women's employment in ethnic enterprise.

Operational Constraints

In addition to the racially discriminatory labour market, many Asian entrepreneurs face a further set of constraints that lock them into the least well rewarded sectors of industry. This is Jones's third point. Asians tend to concentrate on particular sectors like clothing, retailing and catering because it is only low-yielding sectors like these that offer openings to entrepreneurs with few business resources. The occupation of already congested market niches is self-defeating, yet much new business formation is accounted for by recently redundant manual workers entering such sectors because of the low barriers to entry and the minimal skill requirements. Since market demand is largely satisfied by existing firms, this leads to fierce competition in the 'dog eat dog' sector of the market.

Although this is a general tendency affecting entrepreneurs of every ethnic group, Jones makes the point that Asians are especially prone to entanglement in these over-crowded markets, " Starting ... from a previous history of low waged work and/ or unemployment, they are more likely than most to lack personal savings or other assets which might be turned into starting capital " (1992: 13). This dire position is often exacerbated by a lack of training, experience and skills. Discrimination by banks and other key agencies forestalls the pursuit of other options (Ward, 1987). Consequently, Asians seek businesses which demand the least of these resources, and these almost inevitably are the least well-rewarded.

The survey and the case study evidence provides rich information to support these general points. Many Asians entering the clothing industry in the West Midlands had few resources to draw on. They relied on redundancy payments, savings or money borrowed from within the community. Consequently, they found themselves competing with too many others at the lower end of the market. This was compounded by their lack of managerial expertise, skills and training. Few employers had experience of managing or running any kind of business. Most were redundant manual workers or former machinists.

In the cases of many employers in this sector, such constraints were accentuated by the role of agents. At least five companies in the current study used agents to sell their products. Although the proprietors using agents would have liked to have established a direct trading relationship with the end customer, they did not do so for two reasons. Firstly, they believed that they did not possess the necessary marketing skills to establish direct links with retailers. Secondly, there was a feeling that retailers would not deal directly with companies like theirs. It was felt that Asian firms were perceived as unreliable, low standard and exploitative. Hence using white agents with access to buyers from large retailers was a necessary strategy in the quest for larger orders. Chainstore buyers knew of the existence of these companies since it was customary for them to send their quality control personnel to these firms to inspect the merchandise. Yet the buyers still appeared unwilling to contemplate a direct trading relationship.

The problems of sectoral over-concentration are closely paralleled by spatial constriction. The geographical distribution of Asian enterprise in Britain tends to reflect the pattern of the Asian population, which leads to an intensive concentration of businesses in some of the most disadvantaged locations, the West Midlands being a prime example. Firms within inner city areas are subject to a hostile commercial environment with low income markets, poor premises and security and insurance problems being widespread. Although these problems beset most inner city firms,

Asian entrepreneurs are likely to be more exposed simply because they tend to be concentrated in these areas. The result is the creation of 'ethnic enclaves' (Auster and Aldrich, 1984). The causes of this commercial segregation can be traced to the processes of residential segregation, operative since the 1950s, which acted to confine Asians to the least desirable areas of the housing market (Rex and Moore, 1967). Jones (1992:14) reinforces this point, " Residential exclusion has had dire consequences for their economic opportunities, a principle which applies as much to self-employment as employment."

Given this background of racial disadvantage, it is clear that self-employment for minority groups, "... is not just a manifestation of self-help and belief in competition ... in many ways, it is a measure of desperation" (Mitter, 1985: 59). Racism, in its various guises, plays an important role in shaping the terrain upon which minority firms have to operate. It is racism that pushes minority groups into self-employment in the most vulnerable of industries, the most competitive of sectors and the poorest of regions. Moreover, racism keeps them there, the constraints serving as a brake on their development into more lucrative areas of activity.

Family, Gender and Culture

Ethnicity as a Resource

Despite the pervasiveness of racism, an alternative explanation of the rise of minority enterprise has developed which is in virtual opposition to accounts stressing the centrality of racism. This approach has its roots in what Phizacklea (1984) terms 'the sociology of ethnic relations school'. In essence, this approach minimises the view of the migrant/ immigrant as an object of racism, discrimination and exploitation and concentrates upon the ways in which ethnic ties can be used as a resource. This 'resourcefulness' is seen to be of crucial significance in explaining the rise of minority enterprise.

The approach accords primacy to ethnic solidarity and, in the case of Asians, would suggest that 'cultural' features like the ideology of self-help, the operation of fraternal networks and the importance of the family unit are integral to the development of minority enterprise. Werbner's (1984) account of Pakistani entrepreneurship in the Manchester garment trade is typical of this approach. Werbner claimed that the success of

Pakistani entrepreneurs depended to a high degree on 'trust' which is needed to facilitate the extension of credit, expedite transactions and serve as a form of guarantee. Trust is generated via ritual kinship ties, 'through the evocation of moral bonds specific to the members of the group and excluding outsiders' (1984: 168). The source of 'absolute trust' is the family unit which is seen to function jointly for the common good. Members of the family are expected to provide labour for the business and exemplify the Pakistani ethos of self-sacrifice, self-denial and hard work in order to ensure its success.

Studies like Werbner's and others in the tradition of the sociology of ethnic relations school provide a useful service in highlighting the fact that migrants/ immigrants are neither passive nor victims and can actively deploy their particular cultural resources to their advantage. However, when seeking to explain ethnic entrepreneurship, such theories underestimate the impact that racial discrimination in all its forms may have on the development of ethnic groupings and the reliance on 'community' resources for survival. If opportunities for mainstream employment are not open to ethnic minorities because of racism, 'then the adaptation of available skills and resources within a particular group to alternative income generating mechanisms is a reasonably predictable outcome' (Phizacklea, 1990: 85).

Women - the Real Resource

A further problem of the 'ethnicity as a resource' approach is the manner it which it conceptualises 'family labour'. Central to this strategy of enterprise is the availability of a supply of cheap, family and community labour which is deemed necessary to establish and sustain these usually labour intensive industries. Phizacklea makes the point that extant theories, by stressing the importance of family and community labour in establishing the competitive advantage of such firms, ignore the gender specific mechanisms of subordination that generate a supply of low paid female labour,

" What is usually glossed over is the extent to which family and community labour is female and subordinated to very similar patriarchal control mechanisms in the workplace as in the home " (1990: 87).

The use of wives and daughters as unpaid labour was common in the firms visited by Phizacklea and equally evident in the current study. The employers surveyed all used female members of their family in some capacity within the firm. Usually, the wife or the daughter of the proprietor would supervise the machinists in addition to performing the role of an operative herself.

In company A, the wife of the proprietor and his two daughters-in-law were all involved in the running of the family business. For a number of years, the proprietor's wife virtually ran the family retail business (an offshoot of the manufacturing operation). Despite her central role in this enterprise, she was not paid a direct wage. She was allocated a sum of pocket money by the proprietor, yet it was still the 'family business'. The daughters-in-law spent most of their time supervising a group of machinists (who worked in premises attached to the proprietor's home in a different location from company A). They were responsible for ensuring that everyone was supplied with work, looking after administrative matters and working as machinists themselves. In addition to these tasks, the daughters-in-law were expected to shoulder the domestic responsibilities of the household, which, given the fact it was a fairly extensive extended family, were considerable.

The 'wages' that they received for performing this bewildering array of functions consisted of whatever they earned on piece-rate as machinists. This was often negligible since most of their time was taken up on jobs other than sewing. It was expected that their husbands or mother-in-law would provide them with an allowance for personal expenditures.

Despite the low level of direct wages, the three women (the proprietor's wife and the two daughters-in-law) played a crucial role in the day-to-day management of the business' financial resources. For example, the takings of the various parts of the family business would be left with the proprietor's wife for safekeeping. Other than taking money out for household expenditures, she was not supposed to do anything with these funds. In reality, however, she played an active role in the management of these resources. When, for example, Sol, who ran a separate clothing manufacturing business, found his company temporarily short of funds, he would turn to the proprietor's wife. She would usually respond by transferring cash from company A or the family's wholesale operation, which was managed by Bas. A similar scenario would come into play if one of the others required short-term finance. Given the financial ebb and flow of typical clothing companies, such transactions were quite frequent and often involved continual negotiation between the proprietor's wife and the other parties concerned.

The daughters-in-law were responsible for negotiating, calculating and paying the wages of the machinists. They too would often be involved in the handling of the company's financial resources when it came to the payment of wages. They would bargain over the rate for the garment, responsibility for mistakes and the allocation of work. Yet, despite this immersion in the day-to-day financial matters of the business, they had little responsibility for the overall management of company resources.

In company C, the dynamics of patriarchal control were again quite evident. The extensive familial involvement within the company was noted in chapter one. The supervisors, who were the spouses of the men in management, were expected to perform a range of tasks other than sewing, yet it was only for their sewing that they were paid. One of the supervisors, for example, spent much of her time making journeys to and from the cutting room where she would either complain about the cutting, enquire about the order of certain lines or collect work for the machinists. Another supervisor often found herself bound up in the time-consuming process of producing sample jackets and, as a consequence, had little time to devote to sewing at piece-rate. Moreover, at lunch-time in company C, it was 'customary' for one of the women members of the family to cook lunch for the rest of the family. The women took turns to do this. Hence, whoever was performing this task had to forgo her piece-rate measured work time and an element of her lunch time.

Women working under such circumstances, where they receive nominal wages or no wages at all, are in a position which reproduces dependency in a similar way to that of domestic labour (Westwood and Bhachu, 1988: 6). Despite the central role of women family members in the day-to-day management of many of the firms' affairs (as was the case in companies A and C), they had no formal role in decisions relating to company policy or strategy. Bhachu (1988) makes a similar point in her account of the circumstances in which Sikh women could influence decisions on family resources. Although women's participation in paid employment in the open labour market was accompanied by greater 'egalitarianism' between Sikh men and women, once women withdrew from such employment to work in the family business, they were drawn back into the reproductive sphere which served to reinforce patriarchal relations.

The notion of 'family women' has been further reinforced by the impact of immigration legislation, which imposed constraints upon the terms on which Asian women could enter British labour markets (Phizacklea, 1990:96; Westwood and Bachu, 1988). Many minority women did not enter Britain as 'free labourers' seeking to operate in an open labour market. Rather, they came in as 'family women', entering ostensibly for the purposes of marriage or joining their families. As a consequence,

" Family businesses have been able to access minority women's labour power through the mediations of kinship and an appeal to ideologies which emphasise the role of women in the home as wives and mothers and as keepers of family honour " (Westwood and Bhachu, 1988: 5).

This general contention was supported by evidence from the current study. In company A, the two daughters-in-law mentioned above both entered the country for the purposes of marriage. In company B, fifteen machinists were asked why they had come to this country (most of the workforce and management were born in India). Four machinists entered Britain to join their families while eleven came here to get married. Within company C, another fifteen machinists were asked the same question. Two had come to join their families whilst thirteen had entered with the intention of getting married. Since most workers and employers questioned in the survey stage were also born in India, it is quite likely that this is a fairly widespread phenomenon, supporting Phizacklea's contention that "familial ideologies have been usefully brought into play in ensuring the viability of a particular economic form, that of labour intensive business". But, as Phizacklea goes on to point out, "these ideologies must be understood within a context of family immigration or reunion that has taken place within a framework of racist and sexist practices - practices that are built into the fabric of immigration legislation" (1990: 89).

Mitter, whilst not neglecting the impact of racism, immigration and unemployment in fuelling ethnic business, also stresses the importance of familial ideologies in explaining the survival of the sector, " The ideology of the extended family among Asians, or of the village and ethnic loyalty among Cypriots, provides the ideal situation for recruiting a docile and cheap - and overwhelmingly female - labour force " (1985: 55). The integration of immigrant women into the capitalist system is bound up with what are regarded as the 'traditional values' of the immigrant communities. These values mean that the employment relationship tends to be regarded as a traditional obligatory relationship rather than a pure contract. The studies by Hoel (1982) and Anthias (1983) illustrate these 'obligatory' features and the way in which they work to the advantage of male manufacturers. In her account of Greek-Cypriot community involvement in the rag trade, Anthias illustrates how minority men manage the disadvantage that they face in securing mainstream employment. They attempt to overcome this disadvantage by embarking upon small-scale entrepreneurial activity not least because of their capacity to exploit Greek-Cypriot women.

Anthias asserts that the intensive use of female labour is underpinned by an ideology that emphasises the importance of family and the community. The patriarchal value system that is so much a feature of this community extends to the sphere of work, and in doing so, exerts an important influence over the shape of work relations. The actual manipulation of the labour force involves an assertion of shared class interests which is possible on the basis of shared ethnic loyalty and honour. Hence ethnicity is used to obscure the exploitative nature of the capital-labour relationship.

Hoel's study of Asian 'sweatshops' in Coventry attempted to show how employers used aspects of Asian culture to reinforce their control over Asian women workers. Hence, the relationship of servility, subservience and passivity that is evident between men and women in the Asian community was, she argues, reproduced to an important extent at the workplace. The women were 'frightened' of management, a major source of this fear being the range of pressures that employers could bring to bear on them through male relatives and the rest of the community in the event of 'trouble' (1982: 86-90). Management's apparent ability to use the culture was an important factor in them being able to ruthlessly exploit their workforce.

The studies by Hoel and Anthias pointedly illustrate that the survival of ethnic enterprise is predicated upon the exploitation of minority women and to the extent that ethnicity is a resource, it is a resource for migrant men. In highlighting the plight of minority women in these situations, the studies provide a much needed empirical corrective to the gender blind accounts of ethnic business. Despite the pervasiveness of the 'family firm' label, labour power in this context is clearly gendered.

However, in performing this function, such studies run the risk of underestimating the extent to which ethnicity can be used as resource for minority women as well. Despite references to 'extra' economic elements of employment in minority firms, the 'social' dimension of the employer/ employee relationship and the importance of 'obligation', the beneficiaries of these features seem invariably to be the men in management. If ethnicity is to be seen as a fluid and dynamic concept, then it should also possess the potential to serve as a resource for women as well as men. In short, can women as well as men use ethnicity as a resource?

Ethnicity - A Resource for Women

Westwood and Bhachu (1988), Wilson (1978) and Parmar (1982) have all demonstrated that the image of Asian women as naive, passive and subservient is flawed as well as racist. Wilson's account of the Grunwick dispute, for example, illustrates the tenacity with which Asian women resisted a brutal management. The contributions to the volume edited by Westwood and Bhachu show minority women to be active subjects who call upon resources that include their ethnic and cultural contexts in their homes and at the workplace. To this end, Bhachu (1988) records the growing influence of Sikh women in managing resources and Westwood (1988) points up the 'militancy' of Gujerati women in a clothing factory.

These studies illustrate the point that Asian women do not necessarily suffer racism and the more restrictive interpretations of 'ethnicity' in the passive way that is sometimes portrayed. Rather, they draw upon their own resources in an attempt to come to terms with their environment. Parmar makes this point succintly,

" Asian women have developed their own forms of resistance, articulate their own ideas about British society and rely on their historical and cultural traditions as a means of support " (1982:236).

Parmar provides a useful account of the long tradition of Asian women in resistance and charts the numerous struggles that they have been involved in. Asian women bring with them a rich and varied history of culturally specific forms of resistance which cannot be properly understood within Eurocentric frameworks that conceptualise struggle in terms of trade union activity and participation in industrial action. The Asian community relies heavily on its own community cohesiveness in battles against employers. The Grunwick dispute and the strike at Imperial Typewriters in 1974 provide examples of this. In the struggle at Imperial, a major source of strength was the fact that the workers on the shopfloor inside the factory comprised a network of friends and relatives. This network enhanced solidarity both inside and outside the factory and provided material and moral support to the strikers and their families. These women were primarily Asian women from Uganda (Parmar, 1982: 264).

Parmar's conception of 'resistance' seems primarily to involve set-piece battles that workers were engaged in against management. When used in this manner, the term resistance would seem to be appropriate. Workers involved in the disputes at Grunwick and Imperial were clearly 'resisting' management in a conscious and deliberate fashion. However, at the level of every day social relations on the shopfloor, its usage cannot be regarded as entirely unproblematic. Westwood, for example, tries to demonstrate the ways in which Gujerati women in Stitchco could '... generate a powerful resistance to work discipline and the exploitation of capitalist relations' (1988: 106). This is attempted by highlighting particular incidents where the women pretended not to understand management instructions and where they pressed their union to push management to allow them to wear sarees and grant them a day off for Diwali (the Asian 'festival of light'). While not denying the significance of such actions, which indeed were similar to some that occurred on shopfloors within the case study firms, it is doubtful whether they can be seen as evidence of coherent and deliberate 'strategies of resistance'.

In making this point, there seems to be an interesting parallel with the debate on the problematic nature of 'control versus resistance' view of shopfloor relations alluded to earlier. In that discussion, it was contended that management do not simply exert 'direct control' against which workers develop 'strategies of resistance'. Rather, there is always a negotiation of order, although in a definite material context. A similar point can be made in relation to the question of ethnicity. Management cannot simply use ethnicity to further their 'control', and workers do not always suffer as a consequence of it. Ethnicity too is a dynamic concept that involves negotiation. Moreover, its negotiation is not always on management's terms.

Evidence from workplaces investigated here helps to dismantle the myth of passive and powerless Asian women. The previous chapters have all shown the women in the case study companies to be active, assertive and well capable of taking action to manipulate their environment. It was evident that women were integral to the organisation of work on the shopfloor, active in negotiating the rate and capable of exercising considerable discretion over the pattern of working. The task here is not to show that women were strong. Rather, it is to illustrate the ways in which women, as a cultural collectivity, were able to draw upon their ethnic resources for their own ends. In particular, the significance of 'honour', age, background and ceremonies will be considered using evidence from the case study companies.

'Honour' - Safe for Women

Josephides (1988), Ladbury (1984) and Mitter (1985) all make reference to the point that ethnic firms provided minority women with a 'safe' environment to work in. This environment was 'acceptable' to Cypriot and Asian menfolk because it was a familiar setting. Most of the workers were recruited through personal recommendation and, as a consequence, were of the same background and known to the family and the community. In such a setting, the 'Filotimo' or 'Ijjat' (honour) of the women could be protected (Mitter, 1985). By offering a 'safe' environment, family firms were invoking familial ideologies in an attempt to provide women with a route to overcome the contradiction between the need to use women's labour power to generate material resources in the household and the need to reproduce the honour of the family (Josephides, 1988). Minority women could work in such places without risking damage to their reputation and, therefore, the reputation of their families.

The implication of working in a 'safe' environment is that again it is men, in the home and at the workplace, that benefit. In Hoel's study for example, employers were able to use pressure from the community to buttress their harsh management regimes. If workers complained about the terms and conditions, it would reflect badly on those who had introduced the women to the employer. The husbands, fathers or uncles of workers would be contacted by employers should a problem arise with someone deemed a 'trouble-maker' (1982: 89). Hence community pressure, which stemmed from the needs of Asian men to meet obligations and preserve 'honour', served to constrain women workers and reinforced their subordinate position in employment.

While not wishing to deny the potency of the types of pressures outlined by Hoel, there is a case for arguing that it represents a partial and one-dimensional view of how cultural forces beyond the workplace are interpreted on the shopfloor. The potential for features like 'trust', 'honour' and 'obligation' to get in the way of managerial autocracy and work in women's favour were not explored.

The employers in the case study firms examined here could not arbitrarily admonish women workers. To do so would mean that the employers ran the risk of 'dishonouring' the women which would bring with it the possibility of reprisals from the male members of the woman's family. It would also mean that the proprietor would run the risk of being labelled a 'bad employer', which could possibly lead to other women being unwilling or prevented from working for him, a fact of which Sig of company B was well aware,

" If we swore or shouted at them, word will go round this area as fast as anything that we treat our women bad. You know what Indians aren't allowed to do at work."

The proprietor of company A would regularly hurl quite virulent invective at male workers. However, he would be careful not to do so in his dealings with the few women (usually homeworkers) that worked for him. On a particular occasion in company B, Sig was complaining that the machinists were making a 'high' number of 'mistakes' on the order that was currently being processed. Sig was critical of certain machinists whom he believed were responsible for 'mistakes'. He was asked why he put up with it,

" With a bloke, you can tell him to piss off, but what can you do with a woman. What we should really do is go into their room and give them a bollocking but we don't because we're too shy and out of respect."

The notion of being 'too shy' and 'respect' in this context can be seen to be an illustration of Sig's awareness of the nature of gender relationships in the firm and in the wider community, and the consequences of overstepping the mark.

In recognition of the nature of gender relationships and the importance of honour in the wider Asian community, the men and women were separated in the workplace. In all the companies visited during the survey stage of the study, and in most from my own experience, the men were separated from the women, usually by means of a specially created partition. It was very rare that men entered the machinists' shopfloor. Indeed, when machinists in companies B and C were asked what they thought about management, most claimed that they had very little contact with them. 'They hardly ever come in here', commented one woman in company C.

In an important sense, this was a 'safe' environment: an environment in which the women were free from the spectre of racism, the 'problem' of communicating in a different language and, to a significant extent, the direct control of men. The pervasiveness of racism had pushed them into this setting, but at least it was a setting that had a certain familiarity and was one that they could shape. And shape it they did.

This physical divide literally afforded the women the space to mould their own working environment. In the case study companies, relatives and friends sat next to each other, they had lunch at their work stations if they chose to do so and engaged in conversations with colleagues whenever they pleased. The 'banter' level was always high. They had breaks when they wanted. In company B, they even had a settee on the shopfloor with one machinist commenting that when she was tired, she would have a 'lie-down for ten minutes'. The music playing was of their own choice, which usually involved religious services in the morning and 'popular' Asian songs for the rest of the day. Children were often to be seen next to or helping their mothers, a particularly frequent occurrence during school holidays.

In essence, the women used this culturally sanctioned separation, which was deemed necessary to preserve 'honour', to define the contours of the shopfloor. 'Safe' in the knowledge that men were restricted from entering this arena, they had used this culturally afforded discretion as a resource to determine the shape of their own setting.

Age - Attachment to the Culture

The age of the women in the case study companies drew particular significance from its cultural context and, in doing so, contributed to the dynamics of relations on the shopfloor. Phizacklea and others have pointed to the fact that the many constraints that first generation Asian immigrant women have had to endure have left them with a determination to prevent their daughters from suffering a similar fate. Mitter claims that these Asian women provide a cheap and pliant labour force as do Ladbury and Josephides in the case of first generation Cypriot women. The implication is that first generation immigrant women have been and still are prepared to endure harsher conditions than the younger generation of ethnic minority women. This endurance is due to a lack of alternatives and the stronger attachment of this generation to their particular culture.

The constraints imposed by the lack of alternatives is beyond question, but does a stronger attachment to the culture necessarily work in favour of management ? The age profile of the women working in the case study companies reveals that most of the women employed were first generation immigrants. The overwhelming majority of women in companies B and C were over the age of thirty-five, with only two out of a total of forty being in their twenties. It would be fair to say that women of this generation had a stronger attachment to their culture than the younger women. But this same attachment to the culture meant that they were quite insistent on the physical divide between them and the men being in place, they would not tolerate any verbal abuse from management and they expected their age to be respected. Age conferred a certain status on

Asian women which they expected to be observed. Many of the 'mature' women were approached in an almost deferential way by management, who were often younger than many of the workers.

In disputes with management, it was often the more mature women who were at the forefront of the confrontation, even though they might not have been personally involved in the grievance. This was dubbed 'an informal shop steward system' by Sig of company B. On a particular occasion, some linings of an order that was being processed had not been attached to the garments. Sig looked through his records in an attempt to find out who was responsible. They revealed that it was a machinist whom I call Mind. Sig asked Dor to call for Mind (he would not venture on the shopfloor himself). Instead of Mind coming to see Sig, Bero, an older and more experienced machinist, confronted Sig and demanded to know what the problem was. Sig refused to discuss matter with Bero and again asked Dor to summon Mind. This time Mind did go to see Sig, but she was accompanied by Bero. Although the linings were eventually found in Mind's work-box, Sig was reproached by Bero for 'picking on' Mind and she warned him to 'leave her alone'.

This issue of 'representation' was complicated further by the presence of families on the shopfloor. Employers interviewed in the survey stage of the study claimed that a significant number of their workers on the shopfloor were related to each other. In the three case study firms, there were relatives working together on the premises. There were cousins, auntsand nieces, mothers and daughters and mothers-in-law and daughters-in-law. It is possible to view this extensive family presence as both a resource and a constraint. The elders in the family could monitor the activities of younger family members. One machinist in company B, for example, said " I work here because my Mom works here. With the generation change, she thought it would be safer to work here." Management arguably benefit from such attitudes since the family can be used to attract much needed labour and as a possible additional means of control.

However, in the case study firms, it seemed that familial presence on the shopfloor was more of a constraint upon management than a resource, a point not lost on Sig of company B,

'They've set up their own family units in there. If you ever did sack one, you would get two or three threatening to walk out straight away'.

On a particular occasion, one of the machinists in company B came into the cutting room and removed two bundles of work, one for herself and one for her daughter.

'Look at that' Sig exclaimed, 'It's like the bloody Godfather in here, they all look after their own. She's taking a bundle for herself and a bundle for her daughter even though the daughter hasn't finished her work'.

Shaping the Culture

It was noted in chapter four that both companies B and C had a core of long-term employees. The fact that the women in the case study companies had been working for these firms for so long (over ten years in many cases) and they had arrived in similar circumstances seemed to be important in forging tightly knit groups in the respective firms. The women were around the same age, they came to Britain to get married, they got their jobs through each other, they lived in and around the same area and they were of the same caste (Jats). These factors combined to create a very strong identity amongst the women, and any threats to this community cohesiveness were not accepted quiescently, as the 'problem' of recruitment in both firms illustrated.

Management in companies B and C bemoaned the 'shortage of labour', yet in company C, a large number of trainees, of various ethnic backgrounds, left the firm after a few days on the shopfloor. The point was made in chapter four that an important reason for this rapid turnover was their inability to fit into the established pattern of production. However, an equally potent reason was their inability to access the long established culture of the existing machinists.

In company B, management conceded that recruitment was in the hands of the machinists. It was they who appeared to be in control of bringing in workers to the firm. On two separate occasions, workers recruited by management were effectively 'forced out' by the existing workforce. In the first instance, the woman recruited was a West Indian. According to Dor, the supervisor, 'She was a smashing girl and a good worker too, but this lot would not let her stay'. The recruit on the second occasion was a Muslim. The machinists complained about the work of the newcomers and were slow in passing work on to them.

However, on other occasions, the machinists had actually brought in workers themselves and trained them in their own time and, therefore, at their own expense. One machinist who joined the firm a year ago under such circumstances commented, 'I'm not frightened of management, I'm more frightened of the machinists'. In the case of this newcomer, members of the existing workforce took it in turns to train her on different operations, and when she made 'mistakes' they would help her out. Management were not involved in the recruitment or development of her as a machinist. Remarking on the machinists' control of entry into the firm, Sig mused,

> 'It's like the old newspapers in Fleet Street. The only way you got a job was if you knew someone there. It's a closed shop here - If they don't like you, they'll get rid of you. it doesn't matter what management says. They'll irritate you so much that you'll have to go'.

Understanding the Language (or not)

The use of language was a further culturally specific means of workers influencing shopfloor outcomes. Westwood relates an incident in StitchCo when one Gujerrati woman used this particular ethnic resource in an encounter against management. This occurred when the machinist in question pretended that she could not understand instructions (which were in English) for new, more intensive production targets. Her refusal to work to these targets was supported by the rest of the machinists. Westwood claimed that this 'strategy' was used by Asian women in the factory 'whenever it seemed appropriate' (1988: 113).

Notwithstanding the earlier expressed concerns about 'strategy' and 'resistance', the use of language and the feigned non-comprehension of English and simple instructions were undoubted resources which machinists in the current study drew upon. When undertaking the survey, it was noted that all employers bar one held machinists individually responsible for mistake rectification and claimed that they enforced repairs without payment. In the exception to this case (the only non-Asian employer in the sample) the owner would have liked to enforce this policy but was unable to apparently because of his inability to speak Punjabi (which was the mother tongue of his machinists). The machinists collectively prevented him from tracing the work back to individuals by switching the codes on the bundles of work. This made detection impossible. When the machinists were confronted by the owner, they pretended not to comprehend English. Repairs then had to be undertaken by the supervisor who was paid on a day-rate basis.

In company B, the machinists often hurled abuse at their white supervisor, Dor. I could understand what they were saying, but it was obvious that Dor could not. Throughout the day, the women made disparaging remarks about the 'gori' (white woman) in their mother tongue. Dor became the butt of their frustration when work was short, items went missing, garments were poorly cut or when there was something wrong with the machines. The authority that, in the words of Sig, 'the white woman' was supposed to have over this group of machinists was clearly not evident. When, on an occasion noted in chapter four, a particular machinist walked out because she would not work on the garment that Dor had asked her to, no support was given to the supervisor. The matter was resolved by the older machinists, in conjunction with management, visiting the house of the worker in question to persuade her to come back and promising to 'sort Dor out'.

Rather than spending her time on surveillance and supervision (which she was supposed to) Dor frequently found herself at the beck and call of the machinists, often to the chagrin of management. One machinist remarked, 'It's a good job that Dor is here. If she wasn't, we would have to fetch and carry the work ourselves'. When Dor was absent, this is precisely what happened. The machinists would collect the work themselves and organise production around the shopfloor. There was no fuss or dispute.

The ploy of 'not understanding' was evident when the management of company C attempted to change working methods by bringing in consultants, an incident noted in chapter five. The machinists, despite their patently high level of skill, claimed that they could not understand the new ways of working. " Our women will never work that way ", claimed Gel.

This same tactic of feigned non-comprehension of seemingly simple instructions was apparent in company B when it came to the issue of 'counting the work'. After the lay of an order has been cut, the various garment parts are batched. On each batch, the cutter will affix a label citing the size of the garment and the quantity. Hence, a label reading 'L/50' will mean that this particular batch of linings, cuffs, pockets or whatever will contain fifty pieces of size large. This batch then goes into the machinists' room. Each operative receives a batch of work. She will write down the amount that she sews in her own book. When the batch has been sewn, the amount noted in the machinist's book should tally with the number cited on the label.

Although this seems quite straightforward, problems do arise on occasions because sometimes the actual number of pieces in the bundle does not correspond with the figure on the label. This occurs because laying up is not a precise process. At the end of a roll of cloth, there is a remnant that is likely to be less than the length of the lay. Rather than discard the remnant, the cutter will put it on the lay and 'overlaps' it with the required length of similar material. It needs to be overlapped so the full garment shape is accommodated by the material (so, for example, the machinist does not end up sewing half an arm or three-quarters of a pocket). When this occurs it is quite likely that a batch of fifty will contain a few pieces in excess of that number. According to Sig, the machinists always seem to know when the number in the bundle is in excess of that written on the label, 'this suggests to me that they count what they sew'.

However, it is also possible that the amount on a batch is less than that stated on the label. This could be due to a flaw in the material which has not been noticed by the cutter or when the cutting is so poor that it is impossible to sew the garment piece properly. When this happens, Sig claims that the women will still write down the amount cited on the label rather than the actual number that they sew. When they have been approached about this matter, they claim that they only write down what is on the label and they do not count what they sew. 'They pretend they're thick but they're really clever' remarked Sig.

Ceremonies

Westwood cites the 'rituals' and 'celebrations' that women in Stitchco participated in as evidence of acts of 'resistance', " The celebrations which surrounded holidays, brides, motherhood and retirement wrested space and time from the production process and offered the women the opportunity to act collectively " (1988: 116). In the context of Stitchco, these activities and their attendant excesses may well indeed have constituted evidence of resistance against an overbearing management. However, in relation to company B in the current study, celebrations cannot be viewed in such a clear-cut fashion, as the following extract from the field notes illustrates,

> This morning four machinists 'pissed off to the temple' (Sig). They did not seek permission to leave and did not inform management of when they would return. They were away for two hours. Sig commented, " They went to the temple, what can you do." A group of machinists visit the temple at least twice a month, and they always go during work time, rarely informing management of their intentions. They seem to view this as a right. The same process applies to weddings. There is a special ceremony before a wedding and this ceremony usually takes place on a Friday and lasts around two

hours. If the wedding involves one of the machinists or one of their relatives, then the women will attend. Management will drive them to the ceremony and bring them back. This is not entirely for philanthropic reasons; the main concern seems to be to minimise disruption to production. Management's apparently relaxed attitude to such occasions seems to stem from the fact that the machinists are paid piece-rate and therefore not paid during such absences. Despite this, Sig is not totally unconcerned since production is lost. Sig claims to have cracked down, contending that management will only allow machinists to attend the wedding ceremonies of close relatives during work time. Only if it is one of the actual machinists that is getting married will the workforce be allowed to attend en bloc. This move has not been totally unpopular amongst the machinists. There is a pressure to attend such events that stems from aspects of Asian culture, " It's like in India, you expect the whole village to come " (Sig). All the machinists were expected to attend even though some did not really want to because of the income that they would lose as a consequence. A management ruling that rendered such occasions out of bounds would solve this dilemma.

In attending these ceremonies, the machinists in company B were not engaging in deliberate acts of resistance. There was no question of management preventing the women from visiting the temple since the visits were purely for religious reasons. The women, in attending the temple, were motivated by religious concerns, and not by any inclination to 'escape' from management. With regard to the weddings, the women were under an 'obligation' to attend, an obligation that stemmed from cultural ties. For some machinists, this obligation could not be regarded as a resource since it affected the level of their earnings. Hence, it was they who asked management to introduce a rule on the criteria for the attendance of such functions. The incident also illustrates the fluidity of ethnicity and highlights the circumstances when it can act as a resource and a constraint.

Conclusion

The purpose of this chapter was to explore the extent to which ethnicity was a significant factor in shaping workplace relations in the West Midlands clothing industry. To do this, it is necessary to relate ethnicity to the racial context in which it functions as well as the particular values and traditions of the minority group. Without an appreciation of this context the dynamics of ethnicity cannot be fully understood. Westwood and Bhachu make this point in relation to minority women,

> 'social relations are articulated within the racism of the social formation of which they are a part, the ethnic context to which they belong, and the dynamic between this context and the British economy' (1988: 9).

Operating within this framework, it was clear that Asians were pushed into the West Midlands clothing sector because of the absence of alternatives. Once in this sector, racism in its various manifestations served to lock them into the most unpromising of circumstances against which they struggled to survive. The market that such firms were in, their geographical location and the discriminatory practices of agents and financial intermediaries inhibited progression towards more profitable markets. Many survive, though this survival is due to the exploitation of cheap female family and community labour rather than the mystical, esoteric values of the Asian family unit. To the extent that these values were a resource, they were a resource for Asian men, who were able to use them to reinforce Asian women's subordinate position in employment. In showing women to be the real resource, the gendered basis of ethnicity was illustrated.

The current study demonstrated the considerable extent to which the unpaid or poorly rewarded labour of women sustained these clothing companies. Women played a central role in organising production and managing the enterprise. Yet the patriarchal basis of 'familial' ideology within Asian culture and the sexist and racist nature of immigration legislation which classified them as 'family women', combined to reinforce their subordinate position at home and at work.

The usefulness of familial ideologies to management was illustrated in the current study and noted elsewhere by Hoel and Anthias. However, this is but a partial presentation of the multi-faceted nature of ethnicity. Asian women have a long history of struggle that stems from their particular background - they do not experience the oppression that they face in a passive way. In short, ethnicity can be put to work for women too. At the level of the workplace, this history of struggle can filter through and shape accommodations on the shopfloor that benefit women. The case study findings highlighted the ways in which their culture obstructed managerial autocracy. Hence the importance of 'honour' in the community may, as Hoel suggests, repress women, but it can also restrain management in their dealings with Asian women workers. First generation Asian immigrants have undoubtedly had to endure many constraints, but they are more strongly attached to a culture that confers status upon age and the separation of men and women at work. Combined with other mechanisms of accommodation such as language and ceremonies, these cultural features can be significant resources for women.

The current study, then, presents ethnicity in a much more rounded way than hitherto has been the case. Ethnicity cannot simply be seen as an aid to management, but neither can it be seen as a buffer for workers. The very fact of belonging to a particular ethnic group appeared to have certain implications. This was manifested in the separation of Asian men and women, deference to age and so on. However, whether these features furthered or hindered managerial autocracy is open to question. Rather, it is open to negotiation. The significance of ethnicity on the shopfloor will be determined by the way in which it is mediated by the traditions and structures at the workplace. This chapter has provided evidence of the dynamic nature of ethnicity and in doing so, serves as corrective to the view that it is always a resource for management. The next chapter, in reviewing the implications of the findings, establishes the connection between ethnicity and the labour process.

7

Summary and Conclusions

This study set out to explore workplace relations in the West Midlands clothing industry, a setting which serves as an important test case for the varying perspectives on workplace relations in small firms. The particular characteristics of the clothing sector in the West Midlands, namely, the very small size of firms, family ownership and Asian dominance, have been used to support competing views of autocracy and harmony in small firms. Three specific issues were considered in order to examine the reality of social relations at work. Firstly, the processes involved in the negotiation of order in small firms. Secondly, the particular role of management in the operation of these firms. Thirdly, the connection between ethnicity and the labour process. Despite the recent interest in industrial relations in small firms, the debates on management strategy and the proliferating studies on 'ethnic enterprise', the issues addressed in the current study have received relatively little attention elsewhere.

The chapter begins by briefly summarising the major themes of the study. The significance of the study for the wider debate on the connection between ethnicity and the labour process is then considered. This is followed by a discussion of the logic behind the particular texture of workplace relations in the West Midlands clothing industry. In the final section the study is located in a more general framework of industrial relations, the issue of 'typicality' is addressed and the general implications of the findings are presented.

Neither harmony nor autocracy was an adequate categorisation with which to grasp the informal, complex and conflictual make-up of the workplace. The findings from the case study firms clearly illustrate the negotiated nature of life on the shopfloor. This was evident, for example, in the way that the shopfloor was organised. The pattern of production generated an array of often contradictory pressures which had to be managed in a manner that harnessed workers' efforts as well as the demands of a volatile market. Management's lack of command over the intricacies of the production system generated further uncertainties. Employers relied to a significant extent on machinists to 'manage' production on the shopfloor, yet the system itself, which was based on specialisation of tasks, encouraged a concern for isolated operations rather than the process as a whole. Moreover, it accentuated the uncertain place of management - responding to the vagaries of the market on the one hand and having to negotiate on the shopfloor on the other. For instance, management could not really predict how long a particular line would take to progress through the shopfloor despite the fact that they often had tight deadlines to meet.

The tensions evident in the nature of shopfloor organisation were reflected in the establishment of the effort bargain. The rate-fixing process, the nature of supervision and the actual pace of work further highlighted the contested and complex nature of the shopfloor regimes. Previous studies of clothing firms have pointed to management domination of shopfloor relations on the one hand and strategies of worker resistance on the other. Such polarised views of workplace relations fail to convey the bargained nature of life on the shopfloor, the extent of mutual dependency between workers and management and the importance of informal accommodations. The case study evidence presented here illustrated the negotiated and contested nature of the effort bargain which again contributed to the uncertainties facing management within the labour process. In line with the studies by Cunnison (1966) and Armstrong et al (1981), clear evidence emerged of the flexibly negotiated nature of the employment relationship in a highly competitive market.

In relation to employers, the uncertain and contradictory nature of the management process, articulated conceptually by Hyman (1987) and Edwards (1986), was patently evident as manufacturers in the West Midlands clothing industry endeavoured to come to terms with the array of conflicting pressures that they faced. The forces of a hostile and unpredictable market had to be accommodated; but the nature of such accommodations did not inevitably take the form of managerial autocracy as is sometimes suggested. It would seem to be economically rational to casualise work and to rely heavily on family labour; the former supposedly allows for 'flexibility' in response to market fluctuations, while the latter should permit fewer problems of control than paid labour. In fact, flexibility and control demanded less simple responses. The rationale for using external labour was that it could be deployed and jettisoned in accordance to the dictates of the market; yet employers were reluctant to let go of such workers for fear of not being able to compete in the 'busy' season. In the case of the family, the 'benefits' of familial domination of management were sometimes attenuated because of their lack of competence coupled with the need to retain them within the business.

The actual layout of the shopfloor further belied notions of simple rationality. Within a narrow view of economic rationality, it would have been sensible to have a functional plant layout. This would have enabled work to flow smoothly up and down the lines of machines. Instead, machines tended to be located in accordance with the whims of the operatives rather than the demands of 'efficiency'. Yet, despite the random nature of shopfloor layout, management still received a steady flow of work; and this was sufficient to stop them from intervening on the shopfloor. Hence, management's toleration of the less than functional plant layout was not without reason.

Hemmed in by having to manage an array of forces which were inevitably in a state of tension, management faced major constraints in pursuing ostensibly 'rational' action. The result was pragmatism or 'muddling through'. In highlighting the constraints that management faced and the way they discharged their functions, therefore, the current study empirically demonstrates the analysis of management offered by Hyman (1987) and Edwards (1986).

The final theme of the study was ethnicity. The role of ethnicity in shaping workplace relations is bound to feature prominently in a sector which is overwhelmingly dominated by Asians. But ethnicity cannot be examined in isolation. To appreciate the significance of ethnicity, it needs to be related to the wider context of racism in which it operates as well as considerations of the particular values and customs of minority groups in question. The rise of the clothing industry in the West Midlands needs to be examined in the light of the racial constraints that confronted Asian men and women as well as the specificities of Asian culture.

Accordingly, it is necessary to understand that Asians in the West Midlands were pushed into the clothing industry because of the absence of opportunity in mainstream employment rather than the possession of any cultural flair for enterprise. Observing employer after employer frantically attempting to balance the demands of a hostile market, an often chaotic system of production, a far from passive workforce and an indifferent banking system for very little reward leads one to the conclusion that few could have freely chosen such an existence. There were rich pickings, but they were for the fortunate few rather than the helpless many. Racism had confined Asians to the least well rewarded sector of the market and continued to thwart their progression into more lucrative areas of activity.

Many employers then struggled to survive in the midst of these forces; but survive they did. According to the sociology of ethnic relations school, this survival is explained mainly in terms of the particular resources that minority groups are able to draw upon, the most important of which is access to 'family and community' labour. In stressing the activity of minority groups, such perspectives serve a useful purpose; but in minimising the impact of racial discrimination, such accounts neglect the fact that reliance on community resources is a predictable outcome of racism. Moreover, community and family labour means female labour. In other words, the labour power upon which minority enterprise is dependent is clearly gendered.

It is this unpaid or poorly rewarded labour that keeps minority enterprise afloat. The case study findings demonstrated the central role that women played in the production and management of the enterprise. Yet sexist and racist immigration legislation classified them as 'family' women and confined them to a subordinate position at home and in employment. This was compounded by the patriarchal nature of familial ideology within Asian culture.

Ethnicity and the Labour Process

The nature of this ideology and its usefulness for minority men in management has been documented in the studies by Hoel (1982) and Anthias (1983). Such accounts tend to give the impression that ethnicity is important in explaining workplace relations but, apparently, only to the extent that it oppresses women. This represents a rather one-dimensional view of ethnicity. Asian women have a long history of struggle that stems from their particular background. The set-piece battles with management described by Wilson (1976) and Parmar (1982) provide vivid testimony to this. What this study shows is that, at the level of the workplace, ethnicity can be put to work for women too. The culture can actually obstruct rather than facilitate managerial autocracy.

The importance of ethnicity in shaping workplace relations in the context of the West Midlands clothing industry has obvious implications for the debate relating to the independence or otherwise of the labour process. Clearly, it is at odds with Burawoy's contention that relations at the level of the workplace are immune from consciousness imported from outside. For Burawoy, what happened inside the labour process was of prime importance - racial divisions within the workforce did not substantially affect activities on the shopfloor. Within the case study firms, ethnicity was shown to cross-cut simple employer-employee relationships, although this does need to be understood in the context of racism within white British society (Phizacklea, 1990).

In order to assess where the current study should be located within the overall debate on the autonomy of the labour process, it might be useful to reiterate arguments at differing ends of the spectrum. At one end, there is the view most forcefully expressed by Burawoy that what happens inside the labour process should be considered of prime importance,

" Consent is produced and reproduced on the shopfloor and is not dependent on legitimacy drummed into people's heads in schools or on character formation in the family. Even in the marginal situations where consciousness does shape behaviour, its specific impact is determined by the worker's position in the production process " (1979: 201).

Towards the other end of the spectrum is the contention that some external forces are simply imported into the workplace. For example, Thompson (1983: 81) claims that it is impossible to understand the distribution of skills, methods of control and organisation of work, different rates of exploitation, or any other factor connected with the labour process without addressing the sexual division of labour.

The present study does not fit neatly into either categorisation. Management and workers came from a particular ethnic background in which certain values were centrally held. At the level of the workplace, this resulted in the separation of male and female workers, deference to older workers, the acceptance of ceremonies and festivals and the centrality of the family. These features helped to mould shopfloor relations and served as both resources and constraints for management and workers alike. The possession of these values did not, however, have a determinate effect on the nature of workplace relations. It did not dispose managers and workers to act in some pre-ordained fashion unquestioningly. Rather, the values were filtered and interpreted according to the prevailing social relations.

Although being Asian and being a member of a particular caste were important factors, in themselves they did not determine behaviour on the shopfloor. On certain occasions, factors within the labour process did appear to override considerations of ethnicity. An example from company A illustrates this point. The cutter of company A, Gee, was not of the same caste as the proprietor, Phu. Indeed, Gee was from a caste regarded by Phu as lowly - there were many occasions, in private, when Gee's caste was pilloried by Phu. Outside the factory, there was very little contact between Phu and Gee (it was not uncommon for Phu to socialise with workers of his own caste). Within the factory, however, Gee played a pivotal role in the running of the business. He had been with the firm since it first started trading and had duly reached a stage where he was regarded as Phu's 'right hand man'. Knowing the detailed workings of the company, he virtually ran the business on a day-to-day level.

Gee's near indispensability to the organisation allowed him scope and discretion that was not available to other workers. For instance, his persistent lateness went unpunished, he would take time off without informing anyone and would often be allowed to use company vehicles for private use. It was not ethnicity that accounted for Gee's position and treatment within the firm. Indeed, Gee's prominence was a source of much tension. Rather, it was Gee's centrality to the business that determined his shopfloor behaviour.

Similar considerations were at play in relationships with machinists in companies B and C. The machinists were not treated as an undifferentiated mass - their position within the skills hierarchy had a significant impact on shopfloor behaviour. Management rarely allowed their most experienced or 'skilled' machinists (usually those engaged on pockets or finishing) to go without work for any significant length of time. They were a scarce resource; their level of skill and importance to the production process was such that they could almost demand to be kept busy on work that was more or less of their choosing. However, in the case of machinists considered 'less skilled' (deployed on tasks such as linings), management were rather more ambivalent, 'If we are not that busy and they [lining machinists] run out of work, we ask them to go home early or take a day off', claimed Sig, a partner in company B. The skills of these machinists were not so scarce; they were not so central to the process of production. Consequently, management could afford to adopt a firmer line with such operatives.

This example again illlustrates the significance of factors like skill despite the undoubted salience of ethnic considerations. Hence although ethnicity was important insofar as it did literally provide a cultural space that machinists could exploit, factors within the labour process also served to shape behaviour on the shopfloor to an important extent.

Westwood offers a similar analysis with regard to the position of women when they enter the workplace,

" All women coming into social production sell their labour power under conditions they do not make. They share a production process and its demands upon them as workers, and they respond to the labour process both as a set of technical relations and as a set of social and power relations " (1988: 108).

Although Westwood presents control and oppression on the one hand, and resistance on the other in perhaps too simplistic a fashion, she does attempt to demonstrate how women on the shopfloor learn to become workers and how they use their resources as both women and workers to make sense of their factory and domestic lives.

One factor that seems to be increasingly influencing the fluidity of ethnicity is the attitude of second generation Asian women. From past experience and the comments of many employers interviewed in the survey stage of the study, it was evident that young Asian women were unwilling to put up with the kind of shopfloor regime to which their elders were accustomed. One employer commented that 'the young Asian girls prefer to work in shops and offices where they can talk to their friends'. It may be that, for these younger women, the positive aspects of attachment to Asian culture exhibited by workers in the current study no longer outweighed the drudgery of machinists' work. First generation women were largely confined to the garment sector because of the complex interplay of racism, lack of knowledge and language skills and cultural considerations. These forces, however, do not remain static. Racism, for example, although still a major constraint on employment opportunities, may be a different, perhaps lesser, obstacle for these younger women than the one that so heavily restricted first generation women. Whatever the reason, the point is that the nature and significance of ethnicity will change and the manner of its interpretation on the shopfloor will duly alter, although the direction and nature of such change is difficult to predict.

This assessment of the connection between external and internal factors is summed up by Edwards,

" The mechanisms of the workplace may be understood as relatively autonomous: 'relatively' because they are not divorced from other areas and because the degree of autonomy varies between workplaces over time; but still 'autonomous' because of the distinctive principles involved " (1990: 134).

In examining the impact of the much neglected influence of ethnicity on the labour process, and also competition, the current study bears out Edwards' three points relating to the 'relative autonomy' of the labour process (1986: 280-281). Firstly, this study has demonstrated how external conditions have been interpreted in the workplace. Contrary to Rainnie's thesis, the study has shown that in relation to competition, for example, autocracy is not the inevitable consequence of a hostile market environment. The impact of 'external' influences whether they be competition, ethnicity or gender, will be mediated by the structures and traditions of the workplace.

Secondly, the case illustrates how workplace relations develop logics of their own. The outcome and future consequences of negotiations and accommodations cannot be prescribed. The behaviour of particular actors and the persistence of seemingly 'irrational' arrangements were often the product of past struggles and had duly developed logics of their own; their direction need not follow a linear or 'rational' path.

Finally, what may appear 'external' to the labour process may well be influenced by patterns of control. Ethnicity, for example, was not interpreted within the factories in some undifferentiated manner - its impact was influenced to an important extent by the traditions and customs of the workplace. The current study then, has established the 'relative autonomy' of the workplace.

Understanding the 'Irrational'

In assessing how order is negotiated, how management operates and the multi-faceted nature of ethnicity at work, it is apparent that workplace relations are constituted by a range of considerations that defy simple labels like autocracy or harmony. It was evident that a number of factors came together to shape the trajectory of social relations at work; and it was a trajectory that was subject to negotiation and re-negotiation. The picture that emerges from this almost continual state of bargaining is one of complexity and diversity. However, in pointing up the variety of tensions that mediate workplace relations and the 'irrationality' of shopfloor behaviour, there is a danger in obscuring the logic that underpins such organisations. After all, companies, whatever their internal make-up, need to be able to compete in order to survive; so what enables them to survive, what is the logic that lies behind the seemingly chaotic organisation of West Midlands clothing firms ? In order to address this question, it is imperative to contextualise workplace relations and so appreciate the range of forces that shape what happens at work.

In the midst of the complexity at the workplace, one point is beyond question - the rationality of most clothing firms in the West Midlands is definitely not that of the flexible specialisation scenario advanced by Piore and Sabel (1984). I have yet to come across a firm that has restructured along these lines in this region. However, there undoubtedly have been recent trends in the market for clothing and developments in retailer strategies which have increased demand for better quality, high fashion garments; and related changes in technology and manufacturing methods have reduced the cost penalty associated with the production of a variety of styles in short runs. But West Midlands clothing firms do not seem to have gone down this route. There is little evidence of such firms competing in terms of better design and quality, as the optimists might have envisaged.

One problem is that this 'virtuous' approach relies crucially on a flexible and multi-skilled workforce, the adoption of new technology and the commitment of workers to efficient and quality-oriented production, factors which might be more problematic than enthusiasts allow for (Hyman, 1988). However, more importantly, the flexible specialisation paradigm represents just one approach to organisation, and a highly dubious one at that (Pollert, 1991). There are a number of ways in which firms operate, and each will exhibit its own rationality. Hence, clothing firms in the West Midlands that did not follow this path, or indeed the alternative intensification of work route, were not somehow aberrant or anachronistic concerns. They too were rational within the constraints facing them.

Garment manufacturers in the West Midlands were in the midst of a highly competitive market that was rendered even more complex by the presence of intermediaries, the seasonal nature of the business and the impact of racism. These pressures were compounded by problems in fabric sourcing and a lack of training and skill within management. Manufacturers, locked into this sector by racism, found themselves with little option other than to cope with these pressures.

Management could not easily respond to these pressures through simple autocracy, however much that they may have wanted to. This was attributable not only to the fundamental antagonism within the employment relationship; it was also due to a recognition of the 'weakness' of management stemming from the vagaries of the market and, in practice, reliance on workers to organise and manage production. The most complex and skilled tasks were still carried out by machinists, and there was little indication of the adoption of new technology. Consequently, the actual process of manufacture and assembly relied on the co-operation and consent of the machinists. Management therefore had to negotiate on the shopfloor as well as handle the uncertainties stemming from the market. Hence in a setting with few workers, an absence of bureaucracy and a harshly competitive environment, the contradictions at the heart of the capital-labour relation were still evident. And employers of necessity had to manage the tensions emanating from this interface.

The complexity of the workplace was exacerbated - but not determined - by the impact of the labour market and ethnicity. Management had to make contingencies for the so-called 'labour shortage', and this had implications for the nature of work allocation and relationships with external labour. For example, the vicissitudes of the market had to be reconciled with the need to keep scarce operatives supplied with work. The significance of ethnicity meant that considerations like family, caste and gender mediated social relations to a significant degree. These features were important and real considerations in managing the workplace; they were not eccentricities that could be disregarded.

It is against this context that the particular dynamics of workplace relations and their rationality must be assessed. There was a mix of factors that operated at the workplace. Shopfloor outcomes, which reflected the particular importance of these factors, were more the product of negotiation than imposition. Workers, by virtue of their skill and ethnic and familial groupings, were in a position to shape their working environment; and shape it they did in both formal and informal ways. The result was constant negotiation around the effort bargain.

However, it is important also to note that this bargaining took place within certain constraints. The most obvious of these constraints was racism. Asian entrepreneurs and labour turned to the clothing industry because there was little else available to them. Their fortunes, as a consequence, were linked - options elsewhere were limited. Hence despite the pervasiveness of politicking on the shopfloor, the machinists would eventually 'get the pieces out'. Production was often pursued in the form of a 'mad dash' rather than in a planned and systematic manner, but at least the order was met, if not quite on time, if not quite according to specification and if not quite in the colours required.

Operating in this manner, workers and employers managed to survive. Workers were not particularly well paid, but the likelihood of work, let alone better rewarded work, elsewhere was extremely remote. Moreover, by operating in an immediate environment free of racism and largely cut-off from men, the women workers were able to carve out and define their particular space at work. They would not jeopardise this relative 'comfort zone' by taking actions that would drastically endanger management's ability to compete.

The rewards for employers were greater than those for workers, but they were far from spectacular. As the survey evidence indicated, management were not well remunerated and there were few signs of great wealth. Many employers claimed that they took home less than £150 per week in wages, and some even suggested that they only received 'expenses'. There were instances of the 'rags to Mercedes' success stories, but the majority of employers had to content themselves with modest estate cars or vans that served as the family vehicle as well as the means of transporting work to and from the homes of outworkers. Moreover, most employers worked long hours and were often actively engaged in the production process, usually in the spheres of cutting and marking. They too were working to survive.

But survive they did. Although clothing companies in general are not noted for their longevity, the case study firms had been in existence for at least ten years. Fashions had come and gone, competitors had come and gone, but these firms were still there. Larger, bureaucratic and more 'rationally' organised firms like Courtaulds, Laura Ashley and Next have either contracted or gone bust, but firms like those in the West Midlands survive and carry on in much the same way as they did a decade ago.

It is undoubtedly the case that clothing firms in the West Midlands could have operated more 'efficiently' and 'rationally'. For instance, they could have moved closer to a 'flexible specialisation' model by adopting a more bureaucratic approach involving work study, new technology and 'enlightened' labour management policies. This, after all, is the standard solution offered by training providers, local authorities, management consultants and others purporting to assist the industry in the task of removing itself from its current position. However, the implementation of such prescriptions would have required fundamental changes to the entire organisation of the workplace. It would have necessitated the abandonment of a modus operandi that, despite its incongruities and inconsistencies, had proved capable of surviving in a hostile environment.

It is true that by operating in this way, the possibilities of growth and greater profitability that 'rational' packages offered were effectively foreclosed. There was little scope for spectacular profits given the market, management and shopfloor organisation of West Midlands clothing firms, not to mention the impact of racism. But the rewards of 'rationality' were far from certain - the process of bureaucratisation was expensive and offered no guarantee of enhanced profitability. Given the highly unpredictable state of the market, any serious move in this direction would be risky and may have had damaging implications for the practices that allowed such firms to compete in the first place.

The reluctance of firms in the West Midlands clothing sector to adopt 'rational' solutions must be seen against this context. Beneath the veneer chaos and disorder lay a sufficiently flexible and viable system of production. It was this that gave logic to the apparent 'irrationality' of the workplace.

Wider Implications

This account of workplace relations in the West Midlands clothing industry is at variance with many features which are considered to be endemic within the clothing industry as a whole. Employers found it difficult to accommodate the myriad pressures confronting them and seemed to be perpetually engaged in the impossible task of balancing forces which were inevitably in a state of tension. Management clearly did not respond by imposing 'direct control', which is allegedly a mode of authority rife in small firms. Workers were able to use the resources emanating from uncertainties within management and their own background to shape their working environment. They were patently not the passive victims of an overbearing management but neither were they necessarily engaged in deliberate acts of resistance. Rather than operating strategies of control or resistance, management and workers alike were involved in a continuous process of struggle, in the sense that they were involved in 'continuous interactions around the extraction of effort' (Edwards, 1990: 129). The dynamics that resulted from such interactions were illustrative of the complex, contested and mutually dependent nature of workplace relations.

The issue of generalisability then arises. Rainnie appears to regard his findings as typical of the nature of industrial relations in small clothing firms. Given the results of the current study, Rainnie's findings do not provide an accurate assessment of what goes on in clothing firms in the West Midlands. Having made this point, however, the West Midlands clothing industry does have particular characteristics. It is an industry comprising very small companies often employing fewer than thirty people and it is dominated by the Asian community. In the light of these and other characteristics can the conclusions have any relevance beyond the boundaries of the West Midlands clothing sector ?

At one level, the studies are indeed a special case. They demonstrate the highly particular ways in which order is negotiated in a specific context. In performing this function, the case studies, nevertheless, contribute some much needed empirical detail to the grand debates on management strategy which have tended to neglect the concrete ways in which workplace relations are shaped.

Despite the specificities and novelty of the case studies, it is still possible to draw some rather more general conclusions. An obvious point would be that it is unlikely that 'control' in small firms is as 'simple' or as 'direct' as Rainnie would seem to suggest. The elements of co-operation that exist alongside conflict within the employment relationship militate against the kind of autocracy that Rainnie describes. Within the case study firms, it was noted that, for example, pressures arising from the market made management aware of the need to keep costs down, but it also served to increase dependence on particular workers who could adapt to continual style changes.

Firm Size, Autocracy and the Market

Where then do the current studies fit ? Can they be located in a more general model of workplace relations ? There are an infinity of dimensions that can be used to discriminate between the nature of workplace regimes. Littler (1982: 41), for example, employs the 'authorship and guardianship of rules' to illustrate the means by which consent is secured in different types of organisation. Edwards (1986: 226) examines workers' approaches and organisation. The purpose here is not to attempt to emulate these comprehensive accounts of workplace classification. After all, the aim of the exercise was to explore particular workplace regimes in a particular context, not to present a definitive typology of organisations. Rather, the intention here is to speculate on some factors which might account for differences between workplaces.

On the basis of evidence from the current study and comparison with other studies in and beyond the clothing industry, it is worth considering the suggestion that autocracy may be related to firm size and market competition. In very small firms, the employment relationship is likely to be characterised by diffuseness, a high degree of informality and consid-erations beyond the cash nexus. At the other end of the spectrum in large firms, the pattern of control is likely to be more bureaucratic/ autocratic and associated with a high degree of regulation. Where market conditions are relatively stable, the nature of the workplace regime will tend to be hegemonic rather than autocratic; the absence of market uncertainty lessens the range of pressures confronting management.

These differing workplace scenarios are explained in more detail below using a range of studies from different sectors and markets. The starting point is Scase and Goffee's (1982) study of 'fraternalism' in very small firms competing in tight market conditions, which is contrasted with Newby's (1977a) 'paternalism'. Remaining with small firms, Deyo's (1989) study of East Asian firms highlights a greater incidence of bargaining - this is categorised as 'negotiated paternalism'.

As firm size increases, there may be a greater tendency towards more rational/ bureacratic forms of organisation. When the market is highly competitive, as in the studies by Rainnie, Westwood and Armstrong et al., for example, there is a greater probability of autocracy. Where the market is stable, the workplace regime, as Burawoy indicates, is likely to be hegemonic.

Fraternalism

Two studies of small-scale employers by Scase and Goffee (1982) and Newby (1977a) illustrate the differences in small firm working relationships and highlight the significance of market competition in shaping workplace relations. In Scase and Goffee's study of small firms in the building industry, workplace relations fell some way short of paternalism, let alone autocracy.

For the particular circumstances confronting small employers in the building industry, a 'fraternal' approach towards workers was considered most appropriate. These circumstances included the very small size of the firms, the nature of the tasks and the volatility of the market. Typically, these firms employed around six workers, which created a situation where poor performance or absenteeism could have a disproportionate effect on productivity. This vulnerability emphasised small employers' reliance on the men working together as 'equals' in a team. In relation to the task, employers continued to see themselves as tradesmen working with and alongside their employees. For them to cease such work would not only lead to an increase in costs but also introduce a hierarchical element into the relationship which could generate resentment thereby reducing the productivity of the employees.

The volatile nature of the product and labour markets also encouraged a more fraternal approach to labour. Within the context of market uncertainty and a tradition of worker autonomy, management concealed their position by emphasising their role as fellow workers. This enabled them to secure the commitment from tradesmen whose work was not susceptible to more direct forms of supervisory control.

It was the combination of these factors that promoted fraternalism,

"The dependence of small employers upon 'indispensable workers', the nature of the work tasks and the unstable and competitive conditions of the market compel the structuring of egalitarianism between employers and employees. Given the conditions under which these businesses operate, fraternalism represents the most feasible means by which proprietors can control and manage labour" (1982: 119).

Hence fraternalism was made more likely by the interaction of the market, very small firm size and the nature of the task.

Paternalism

Newby's study of East Anglian farmers highlights a different approach to the management of the employment relationship. These farmers were even smaller scale employers than those firms studied by Scase and Goffee, yet the dominant mode of authority was paternalism rather than fraternalism. There were two main reasons for this. Firstly, it was highly unlikely that farm workers could ever become farmers. There was more of a hierarchy, more of a division between them than the workers and employers in the Scase and Goffee study. The second reason appeared to be the stable nature of the market. An adverse or particularly volatile market could jeopardise the social obligations upon which paternalism was predicated, but

"the stability given to agriculture by state support ... has ... meant that the economic order upon which their [the farmers'] dominance rests throws up fewer problems to threaten the stability of employer-employee relationships than in most other industries" (1977a: 422).

This relative insulation from market pressures fostered a concern for the more 'social' elements of the relationship between farmer and farm worker. The actual nature of the employment relationship tended to be based on a 'face to face, gaffer to man basis'. Farmers legitimated their authority by the invocation of tradition, social obligation and custom.

Despite the importance of the 'social' aspects, the farmer had a number of mechanisms that served to tie the worker into the paternalist web. The farmer, of course, had the power to 'hire and fire', a resource that was quite potent given the lack of employment opportunities available to farm workers (cf the high mobility of builders in the Scase and Goffee study). Furthermore, farmers were often in a position where they could control housing, either directly through the provision of tied accommodation, or indirectly through their control of rural councils. Yet, farmers rarely operationalised this potential for autocracy. Legitimation by tradition was the preferred and most pervasive mode of authority, primarily because it had proved the most stable.

The agricultural workers' acceptance of, or deference to, such an employment relationship was based on an acknowledgment of this state of dependency rather than a positive affirmation of the workplace regime,

" For the most part ... the agricultural worker has acknowledged his powerlessness and decided to make the best of his inferior situation, contriving to take it somewhat for granted while not necessarily endorsing it in terms of social justice " (1977a: 415).

Furthermore, this conceptualisation of deference as a product of a particular set of social relationships rather than a reference to a facet of workers' personality points up the essential contradiction within paternalism, or the 'deferential dialectic'. On the one hand there is a need to maintain a hierarchical differentiation. This is a differentiation essentially of power which is reflected through the differential control of resources in most aspects of the farmers' and farm workers' lives. On the other hand, paternalism requires the cultivation of identification by defining the relationship as an organic partnership in a co-operative enterprise.

Although the basic antagonism between differentiation and identification could potentially pose a threat to the paternalist order, the tensions stemming from this antagonism are capable of being managed. The nature of this 'tension management' will be a product of the prevailing set of social relations.

Negotiated Paternalism

Within negotiated paternalism, the employment relationship is still marked by a high degree of diffuseness. As with the paternalism of Newby's study, notions of mutuality and obligation are likely to figure quite prominently. However, there is likely to be a greater degree of negotiation, although mostly through informal means. Drawing on Deyo's

(1989) study, it is probable that small firms within the newly industrial-ising countries of East Asia fit into this category.

Deyo (1989) suggests that small firms in countries like Hong Kong and Taiwan that sub-contract to larger factories are characterised by 'patriar-chal' forms of authority. Accordingly, familial and community links play an important role in shaping the workplace, which is regulated by norms of non-economic reciprocity and mutual obligation.

In common with workers in the West Midlands clothing industry, East Asian labour, particularly in small firm settings, appears to have a reputation for 'docility'. However, this stems as much from a lack of awareness of the particular nature of negotiation in such concerns as it does to the absence of conflict. There is conflict, but it tends to be pursued through indirect and personal channels. Familial and community ties play a significant role in regulating what happens at work; and such ties serve to keep wayward employers in line in addition to being a source of authority over workers. Hence employment relations here too are largely determined by informal bargaining, with workers carrying 'their dissent into kitchens, elevators, coffee-houses, and backrooms rather than into the streets' (Deyo, 1989: 161).

Bureaucratic/ Autocratic

Above a certain size of firm however, such traditional and personal means of control tend not to be effective. In larger firms, the scope for informality, negotiation and politicking is severely attenuated, although not totally eliminated. Firms of this size may need to operate more impersonally and bureaucratically. The studies undertaken by Armstrong et al (1981) in clothing and footwear companies, Edwards and Scullion (1982) in hosiery and underwear manufacturers, Westwood (1984) in a clothing factory and Gabriel (1988) in the catering industry were in much large firms that required more bureaucratic and rational systems of control to co-ordinate a much wider range of activities. These studies will now be considered in order to illustrate the link between firm size, autocracy and market conditions.

Armstrong et al focused on the construction of managerial legitimations at the workplace and the processes involved in shaping understandings of the employment relationship. However, the study also provides an insight into the progression towards autocracy and rationality in larger firms operating in competitive markets. Management prerogative here was rarely questioned and their 'logics' tended to be accepted by workers. If, for example, management deemed it necessary to cut piece-work rates in order to remain profitable, workers usually accepted it without question. Although workers did occasionally protest about work arrangements, the size of the firm and its market position had, to a major extent, organised out any real scope for flexibility.

The focus of Edwards and Scullion's study was different but a similar situation could be observed in their examination of the Hosiery and Underwear factories (both employing in excess of 300 workers). For example, the managerial principles were quite simple: the companies were in a competitive industry, and the only way to survive was to maintain price levels, meet delivery dates and sustain a high level of quality and reliability. In terms of the management of the labour process, this resulted in the strict enforcement of discipline on the shopfloor, with supervisors firmly discouraging workers from moving from their work stations and talking to their colleagues.

Westwood's study of StitchCo further illustrates the autocratic organisation of work in larger firms. Workers were discouraged from moving around the shopfloor, their tasks were broken down into component parts and they were continually 'up against the minutes'. Bureacracy, in the form of a conspicuous hierarchy, job evaluation and work study, served to lessen reliance on the machinists' tacit skills. The market environment and firm size appeared again to have a significant effect on the scope for flexibility in the employment relationship. However, it was not totally eliminated. Management still attempted to adopt a personalised approach to workers by referring to them as 'girls', taking an interest in workers' personal lives and employing jokes and humour regularly. Furthermore, workers devised particular means of 'resisting' management.

Where firms are very large and competition is intense, one might anticipate a highly bureaucratic/ autocratic system of authority. McDonalds, which has very strict control within exact procedures, is perhaps an example of this approach. Gabriel (1988) provides an insight into the nature of workplace relations in such regimes via his study of 'Fun Food International', which has several hundred stores in the United Kingdom and is highly ranked among the world's 25 largest catering companies. The workplace was highly regulated,

" The products, the service, the cooking, the seating arrangements, the location of the stores, the technological hardware and software, are all determined according to the principle that there is 'one best way'. The work itself, the storing and unpacking of materials, the cooking, wrapping and presenting of products, the appearance of the staff and the way they address the customers, are all laid down to the smallest detail in rules and regulations " (p 95).

Using R. Edwards's three point control typology, Gabriel suggests that management control in Fun Food was bureaucratic rather than simple or technical. Although Gabriel's use of R. Edwards's rather fragile model is unduly neat and uncritical, the study does indicate the significant extent to which the employment relationship was bound by regulations. However, even in such a regulated environment, 'there were short-cuts, games, little trade secrets and personal touches of the workers [that] represent[ed] a little area of negotiation' (p 107).

Bureaucratic/ Hegemonic

Burawoy's (1979) study of large engineering plants offers an insight into the nature of workplace relations in conditions of relative market stability. The transition from competitive to monopoly capitalism alters the way in which consent is secured at the level of the workplace. Burawoy found that a despotic regime under conditions of intense competition was replaced by the hegemonic organisation of work under monopoly capitalism, with consent predominating over coercion. Among the central features within the hegemonic workplace were the internal labour market and an independent grievance procedure.

Burawoy's counterposing of despotism and hegemony, and coercion and consent is undoubtedly problematic. For example, there has to a negotiation of a certain degree of consent even in a despotic regime. However, the purpose is not to embark on a thoroughgoing analysis of such matters (for a critical appraisal of Burawoy's thoughts on the labour process, see Edwards, 1986: 46-54). Rather, the importance for issues of concern here is that when market conditions are stable, hegemony rather than autocracy is likely to be the dominant mode of authority.

Locating the Current Study

Within this general framework, the most appropriate location for the current study would be 'negotiated paternalism'. The current study was in larger concerns than those of Scase and Goffee and Newby, but were still very much in the small firm category. The market conditions facing such firms were undoubtedly harsh, but the outcome was neither the fraternalism of the Scase and Goffee study nor the autocracy witnessed in Rainnie's cases. Rather, there were a range of mostly informal processes, accommodations and struggles. The uncertainties occasioned by the product market were compounded by uncertainties within the system of production, the supervisory regime and the labour market. It would undoubtedly have been 'rational' to formalise or bureaucratise elements of the firms' operations. For example, the setting of the piece-rate and the system of production could have been organised more 'efficiently'. However, to have done so would have risked disrupting the existing configurations of workplace relations.

Rather than autocracy or deference, the result was a range of approaches involving almost continual negotiations over the effort bargain. Mediating such negotiations were factors like the product market, labour market, the time of the year, caste and culture. These factors would influence the rate-fixing process, the allocation of work, the enforcement of mistake rectification and other aspects of workplace organisation. Ethnicity further shaped the character of the employment relationship, and like the influence of other factors, its impact also had to be interpreted and negotiated.

These negotiations, informal bargains and trade-offs were not planned or coherent. This can be contrasted with the 'militant individualism' that Cunnison (1966) identified in her study of the 'Dee' waterproof garment factory. At 'Dee', workers appeared to have a high degree of bargaining awareness; they engaged directly in individual struggles with managers over the fixing of the weekly wage and matters influencing it such as the piece-rate prices and the allocation of work. The bargaining over effort therefore appeared much more direct and overt than in the current study.

Yet, despite the informality of the negotiating process in the current study, exchanges can, over time, develop logics of their own and may lead to a situation where they threaten they basis of the social order itself. In other words,

> "Custom ... sanctions claims upon those exercising a paternalist mode of control which frequently leads to paternalism being redefined from below in a way that forms the basis of the overthrow of paternalism itself" (Newby, 1977b: 72).

Workers in the current study deemed it their 'right' to take time off when they wanted to; they worked in a manner that they had grown accustomed to and they expected a particular kind of work. These expectations were a continual source of tension. Sometimes they were met, sometimes they were not. Nevertheless, as witnessed with the 'locally rational' system of production, they do pose a potential threat to management.

Despite the tensions inherent within the case study firms, the firms were still in operation. Hence, paternalism, even in this highly negotiated manner, had worked. In spite of the apparent irrationalities and idiosyncrasies, management appeared to 'muddle through'. Consequently, there was a certain logic to the way management proceeded, and that logic was one of managing conflicting pressures. For these employers, like other capitalists, the logic was 'governed by the need to continue the generation of surplus value' (Edwards, 1990: 136).

The foregoing discussion does not in any way constitute an attempt to devise a new typology. This was not the aim of the exercise, and, in any case, typologies are unlikely to grasp the complexities of workplace relations. Neither is it suggested that management impose particular forms of control, whether it be paternalism or bureaucracy. Rather, these studies of firms have been used to illustrate the connection between firm size, autocracy and market conditions. They highlight the trend towards autocracy as firm size increases - larger companies within a competitive market setting appeared to operate in a more bureaucratic/ autocratic fashion. In veering towards autocracy, flexibility became increasingly organised out of the employment relationship.

In presenting the framework in this manner, the implications of the study can be set in a wider context. Although the West Midlands clothing sector does have particular features, the findings overwhelmingly illustrate that workplace relations in small firms are neither intrinsically autocratic nor harmonious. A variety of factors will combine to shape the shopfloor, and amongst them will be the market and firm size. The comparisons with other studies in different sectors and markets points to the growth of autocracy as firm size increases.

It is likely therefore that the processes described within companies in the West Midlands clothing sector are probably 'typical' of ethnic minority-dominated inner city firms operating in competitive markets. Further afield, Deyo's study suggests that similar sorts of relationships are in place in the newly industrialising countries of East Asia. In smaller firms, like those of Scase and Goffee and Newby, the employment relationship is likely to be more diffuse than that in the current study.

As firm size increases, the tendency towards rational and bureaucratic forms of organisation will be more pronounced. The growth of autocracy that accompanies firm size is likely to lead to a highly regulated workplace where the market is competitive; but hegemonic patterns of control are likely to prevail where competition is not intense. However, even in these cases of autocracy and hegemony, order still needs to be negotiated; its scope and flexibility will be reduced but it is unlikely to be totally eliminated.

The problem with Rainnie's account, apart from the tendency to over generalise, was the apparent absence of any room for flexibility. It seemed the a hostile market necessitated autocracy on the shopfloor, with workers apparently passive in the face of an overbearing management. The failure to pick up areas of negotiation in the workplace may have due to a deficiency in the research design, perhaps being too remote from the actual shopfloor. But whatever the reason, studies of firms organised along rational lines and operating in competitive markets, notably that of Westwood, indicate that there is still space for negotiation.

Concluding Remarks

In assessing the more general implications of the current study, three issues may be illuminated. Firstly, potential areas for further research. Secondly, the importance of an appropriate methodology to studying workplace dynamics. Finally, the pattern, or patterns, of control in the West Midlands clothing industry in relation to other firms in the clothing sector. These issues will now be adumbrated.

In terms of future research, two areas seem of considerable potential: the links between family and the shopfloor, and women's shopfloor culture. The current study pointed to the significance of family connections for shopfloor relations. Given that the local industry is dominated by family businesses, this issue is of considerable importance. Although the focus of this study has been workplace relations, it nevertheless contains much evidence to suggest that family-shopfloor links shape the working environment in an important way. The links and tensions within the family, their impact on the family at work and the contribution of the family to the survival of the small firm would seem to be of significance for shopfloor relations. Further research addressing these issues centrally would be useful.

There is also the question of women's shopfloor culture. Westwood among others has tackled this question head on, but the extent to which she is sufficiently sensitive to the specificities of Asian women's workplace experiences is subject to some doubt. This study has addressed particular issues pertaining to the workforce, like the extent to which they could draw upon their culture to shape their working environment. However, there is still scope for a considerable 'painting in' of the detail of Asian women's shopfloor experience. A particular line of inquiry could be the extent to which second generation Asian women relate to their culture and the implications that they may have at the level of the workplace.

The second major issue arising from the findings is the importance of an appropriate methodology. The methodology deployed in the current study enabled insights to be elicited which perhaps would not have been easily accessible to others. As noted in the chapter on methodology, being an Asian man with both a research background and a high level involvement in, and experience of, typical clothing firms in the West Midlands, I was uniquely placed to undertake this enquiry into the dynamics of workplace relations. The resources at my disposal allowed me to gain access to workplace cultures and witness the reality of life on the shopfloor. However, it is not solely social reporting - hopefully, the investigation constitutes a study of workplace relations informed by a consideration of its significance in the wider context. The purely ethnographic studies of women workers arguably lack this critical dimension while Rainnie's study fails to adequately illustrate the complexities of shopfloor behaviour.

The final issue of importance concerns the position of the current study in relation to other firms. Implicit in the speculations on firm size and autocracy is the suggestion that larger firms tend to be organised on a more rational and bureaucratic basis than smaller firms. Where then does the current study fit in vis a vis other studies of clothing firms? It is clearly a rebuttal of Rainnie's suggestion that autocracy is an endemic feature of industrial relations in small firms per se. However, it is equally apparent that the type of control regime identified in the West Midlands clothing industry is not typical of the total clothing sector. The processes involved in the establishment of order are probably common in small firms of this genre, but as the studies of Westwood, Armstrong et al, Edwards and Scullion and even Rainnie demonstrate, the tendency towards rational organisation is more likely in larger firms. This does not mean that negotiation and struggle is eliminated - rather, the scope and form that it takes alters and attenuates the room for informality.

Features like work study, which prescribe work pace and methods, were arguably necessary in the larger firms to secure uniformity and the control of costs, and were made possible by the utilisation of relatively sophisticated techniques. In the West Midlands setting, management often did not have the competence to use such devices, which again served to increase their dependence on the knowledge of workers. The suggestion is not that sophisticated managements in the studies of larger firms devised and implemented a coherent strategy of control whereas in the West Midlands they did not. Rather, it seemed that management needed to have much more bureaucratic and autocratic means of control, just as employers in the West Midlands needed informal workplace relations to survive in a highly competitive market environment.

References

Aldrich, H, T. Jones and D. McEvoy. 1984. 'Ethnic Advantage and Minority Business Development'. *Ethnic Communities in Business*. Ed. R. Ward and R. Jenkins. London: Cambridge.

Anthias, F. 1983. 'Sexual Divisions and Ethnic Adaptation: the Case of Greek-Cypriot Women'. *One Way Ticket*. Ed. A. Phizacklea. London: Routledge and Kegan Paul.

Armstrong, P. 1986. 'Managerial Control Strategies and Inter-Professional Competition'. *Managing the Labour Process*. Ed. D. Knights and H. Wilmott. Aldershot: Gower.

Armstrong, P. 1989. 'Management, Labour Process and Agency'. *Work, Employment and Society*. Vol. 3, no. 3, 307-322.

Armstrong, P., J. Goodman and J. Hyman. 1981. *Ideology and Shopfloor Industrial Relations*. London: Croom Helm.

Auster, E. and H. Adrich. 1984. 'Small Business Vulnerability, Ethnic Enclaves and Ethnic Enterprise'. *Ethnic Communities in Business*. Ed. R. Ward and R. Jenkins. London: Cambridge.

Bell, C. and H. Newby. 1977. (Eds), *Doing Sociological Research*. London: Allen and Unwin.

Bhachu, P. 1988. 'Apni Marzi Kardhi. Home and Work: Sikh Women in Britain'. *Enterprising Women*. Ed. S. Westwood and P. Bhachu. London: Routledge and Kegan Paul.

Birmingham City Council. 1990. 'Fact sheet'. Economic Development Unit, the City Council.

Boissevain, J. 1984. 'Small Entrepreneurs in Contemporary Europe'. *Ethnic Communities in Business*. Ed. R.Ward and R. Jenkins. London: Cambridge.

Braverman, H. 1974. *Labor and Monopoly Capital: The Degradation of Work in the Twentieth Century*. New York: Monthly Review Press.

Bresnen, M. 1988. 'Insights on Site: Research into Construction Project Organisations'. *Doing Research in Organisations*. Ed. A. Bryman. London: Routledge and Kegan Paul.

Brooks, D. and K. Singh. 1979. 'Pivots and Presents: Asian Brokers in British Foundries'. *Ethnicity at Work*. Ed. S. Wallman. London: Macmillan.

Brown, C. 1984. *Black and White in Britain: The Third PSI Survey*. London: Heinemann

Brown, W. 1973. *Piecework Bargaining*. London: Heinemann.

Bryman, A. 1988. 'Introduction: 'Inside Accounts and Social Research in Organisations'. *Doing Research in Organisations*. Ed. A. Bryman. London: Routledge and Kegan Paul.

Bryman, A. 1988a. *Quantity and Quality in Social Research*. London: Unwin Hyman.

Bryman, A. 1989. *Reseach Methods and Organization Studies*. London: Unwin Hyman.

Buchanan, D., D. Boddy and J. McCalman. 1988. 'Getting In, Getting On Getting Out and Getting Back'. *Doing Research in Organisations*. Ed. A. Bryman. London: Routledge and Kegan Paul.

Bulmer, M. 1988. 'Some Reflections Upon Research in Organisations'. *Doing Research in Organisations*. Ed. A. Bryman. London: Routledge and Kegan Paul.

Burawoy, M. 1979. *Manufacturing Consent*. Chicago: University of Chicago Press.

Burgess, R. 1984. *In the Field*. London: Unwin Hyman.

Carr, H. and B. Latham. 1988. *The Technology of Clothing Manufacture*. Oxford: Blackwell Scientific Publications.

Cavendish, 1982. *Women on the Line*. London: Routledge and Kegan Paul.

Clawson, D. and Fantasia, R. 1983. 'Review Essay. Beyond Burawoy: the Dialectics of Conflict and Consent on the Shopfloor'. *Theory and Society*. Vol. 12, no. 3, 671-80.

Collinson, D., D. Knights and M. Collinson. 1990. *Managing to Discriminate*. London: Routledge and Kegan Paul.

Coyle, A. 1982. 'Sex and Skill in the Organisation of the Clothing Industry'. *Work, Women and the Labour Market*. Ed. J. West. London: Routledge and Kegan Paul.

Crompton, R. and G. Jones. 1988. 'Researching White Collar Organisations: Why Sociologists Should Not Stop Doing Case Studies'. *Doing Research in Organisations*. Ed. A. Bryman. London: Routledge and Kegan Paul.

Cunnison, S. 1966. *Wages and Work Allocation: a Study of Social Relations in a Garment Workshop*. London: Tavistock.

Dalton, M. 1959. *Men Who Manage*. New York: Wiley.

Davenport, E. 1992. 'Changing Relationships in the Material World: UK Retailers' Sourcing Policies for Clothing Products'. *Prospects for Industrial Policy in the 1990s: The Case of the British Clothing Industry*. Ed. D. Gillingwater and P. Totterdil. Aldershot: Gower.

Davenport, E., P. Totterdill and J. Zeitlin. 1986. *Training for the Clothing Industry: A Strategy for Local Government*. Unpublished report prepared for the Greater London Council.

Deyo, F. 1989. *Beneath the Miracle - Labor Subordination in the New Asian Industrialism.* Los Angeles: University of California Press.

Dick, B. and G. Morgan. 1987. 'Family Networks and Employment in Textiles'. *Work, Employment and Society.* Vol. 1, no. 2, 225-246.

Edwards, P.K. 1986. *Conflict at Work.* Oxford: Blackwell.

Edwards, P.K. 1988. 'Patterns of Conflict and Accommodation'. *Employment in Britain.* Ed. D. Gallie. Oxford: Blackwell.

Edwards, P.K. 1990. 'Undestanding Conflict in the Labour Process: The Logic and Autonomy of Struggle'. *Labour Process Theory.* Ed. D. Knights and H. Willmott. London: Macmillan.

Edwards, P.K., and H. Scullion. 1982. *The Social Organisation of Industrial Conflict.* Oxford: Blackwell.

Edwards, R. 1979. *Contested Terrain: the Transformation of Work in the Twentieth Century.* London: Heinemann.

Ferner, A. 1985. 'Political Constraints and Management Strategies'. *British Journal of Industrial Relations,* Vol. 1, no. 1, 47-70.

Friedman, A. 1977. *Industry and Labour.* London: Macmillan.

Gabriel, Y. 1988. *Working Lives in Catering.* London: Routledge and Kegan Paul.

Gartman, D. 1983. 'Review Essay. Structuralist Marxism and the Labour Process. Where Have the Dialectics Gone?' *Theory and Society,* Vol. 12, no. 3, 659-69.

Genovese, E. 1976. *Roll, Jordan, Roll: the World the Slaves Made,* New York: Vintage.

Gordon, D. M., R. Edwards and M. Reich. 1982. *Segmented Work, Divided Workers: The Historical Transformation of Labor in the United States.* Cambridge: Cambridge University Press.

Goss, D. 1988. 'Social Harmony and the Small Firm'. *Sociological Review,* Vol. 36, no. 1, 114-132.

Goss, D. 1991. *Small Business and Society.* London: Routledge.

Gouldner, A.W. 1954 *Patterns of Industrial Bureaucracy.* New York: Free Press.

Handsworth Technical College. 1984. *The Clothing Industry in Birmingham.*

Hayden, C. 1992. 'A Case Study of the Clothing Industry in the West Midlands'. *Prospects for Industrial Policy in the 1990's: The Case of the British Clothing Industry.* Ed. D. Gillingwater and P. Totterdil. Aldershot: Gower.

Hobbs, D. 1988. *Doing the Business: Entrepreneurship, the Working Class and Detectives in the East End of London.* Oxford: Oxford University Press.

Hoel, B. 1982. 'Contemporary Clothing Sweatshops. Asian Female Labour and Collective Organisation. *Work, Women and the Labour Market.* Ed. J. West. London: Routledge and Kegan Paul.

Hyman, R. 1987. 'Strategy or Structure ? Capital, Labour and Control'. *Work, Employment and Society.* Vol. 1, no.1, 25-55.

Hyman, R. 1988. 'Flexible Specialisation: Miracle or Myth ?'. *New Technology and Industrial Relations.* Ed. R. Hyman and W. Streeck. Oxford: Blackwell.

Ingham, G. 1970. *Size of Industrial Organisation and Worker Behaviour.* Cambridge: Cambridge University Press.

Jenkins, R. 1984. 'Ethnic Minorities in Britain: A Research Agenda'. *Ethnic Communities in Business*. Ed. R. Ward and R. Jenkins. London: Cambridge.

Jenkins, R. 1984a. 'Bringing it All Back Home: An Anthropologist in Belfast. *Social Researching: Politics, Problems, Practice*. Ed. C. Bell and H. Roberts. London: Routledge and Kegan Paul.

Jenkins, R. 1986. *Racism and Recruitment*. Cambridge: Cambridge University Press.

Jones, T. 1992. 'Ethnic Business and the Post-Fordist Entrepreneurial Renaissance'. *Prospects for Industrial Policy in the 1990s: The Case of the British Clothing Industry*. Ed. D. Gillingwater and P. Totterdill. Aldershot: Gower.

Josephides, S. 1988. 'Honour, Family, and Work: Greek Cypriot Women Before and After Migration'. *Enterprising Women*. Ed. S. Westwood and P. Bhachu. London: Routledge and Kegan Paul.

Kelly, J. 1985. 'Management's Redesign of Work'. *Job Redesign*. Ed. D. Knights, H. Wilmott and D. Collinson. Aldershot: Gower.

Knights, D. 1990. 'Subjectivity, Power, and the Labour Process'. *Labour Process Theory*. Ed. D. Knights and H. Wilmott. London: Macmillan

Knights, D. and H. Wilmott. 1986. Eds. *Managing the Labour Process*. Aldershot: Gower.

Kochan, T., R. McKersie and P. Cappelli. 1984. 'Strategic Choice and Industrial Relations'. *Industrial Relations*. Vol. 23, no. 1, 16-39.

Ladbury, S. 1984. 'Choice, Chance or No Alternative.' *Ethnic Communities in Business*. Ed. R. Ward and R. Jenkins. London: Cambridge

Lamphere, C. 1979. 'Fighting the Piece-Rate System: New Dimensions of an Old Struggle in the Apparel Industry'. *Case Studies on the Labor Process*. Ed. A. Zimbalist. New York. Monthly Review Press.

Lazonick, W. 1981. 'Competition, Specialisation and Industrial Decline'. *Journal of Economic History*, Vol. 41, no. 1, 31-38.

Leigh, R. and North, R. 1983. *The Clothing Sector in the West Midlands*. Report for West Midlands County Council.

Lewis, R. 1988. *The Training Needs of the Clothing Industry in Birmingham and Wolverhampton*. Handsworth Technical College.

Littler, C. 1982. *The Development of the Labour Process in Capitalist Societies*. London: Heinemann.

Littler, C. and Salaman, G. 1982. 'Bravermania and Beyond. Recent Theories of the Labour Process'. *Sociology*, Vol. 16, May, 251-269.

Lupton, T. 1963. *On the Shopfloor: Two Studies of Workshop Organisation and Output*. Oxford: Pergamon

Lloyd, C. 1989. 'Restructuring the West Midlands Clothing Industry'. *New Technology, Work and Employment*, Vol. 4, no. 3, 100-106.

Maguire, 1988. 'Work, Locality and Social Control'. *Work, Employment and Society*. Vol. 2, no. 1, 71-87.

Marchington, M. 1990. 'Analysing the Links Between Product Markets and the Management of Employee Relations'. *Journal of Management Studies*, Vol. 27, no. 2, 111-32.

Mars, G. and R. Ward. 1984. 'Ethnic Business Development in Britain'. *Ethnic Communities in Business*. Ed. R. Ward and R. Jenkins. London: Cambridge.

Mawson, J. 1988. 'The West Midlands Clothing and Textile Industry: a Sector Review'. Birmingham: West Midlands Enterprise Board.

Mitter, S. 1985. 'Industrial Restructuring and Manufacturing Homework'. *Capital and Class*. No. 27, 37-80.

Moore, R. 1977. 'Becoming a Sociologist in Sparkbrook'. *Doing Sociological Research*. Ed. C. Bell and H. Newby. London: Allen and Unwin

Newby, H. 1977a. *The Deferential Worker: A Study of Farm Workers in East Anglia*. Harmondsworth: Penguin.

Newby, H. 1977b. 'Paternalism and Capitalism'. *Industrial Society: Class Cleavage and Control*. Ed. R. Scase. London: Allen and Unwin.

Nolan, P. 1983. 'The Firm and Labour Market Behaviour'. *Industrial Relations in Britain*. Ed. G. Bain. Oxford: Blackwell.

Nolan, P. and W. Brown. 1983. 'Competition and Workplace Wage Determination' *Oxford Bulletin of Economics and Statistics*, Vol. 45, no. 3, 269-287.

Nolan, P. and P. K Edwards. 1984. 'Homogenise, Divide and Rule: an Essay on Segmented Work, Divided Workers'. *Cambridge Journal of Economics*, Vol.8, no. 2, 197-215.

Oakley, A. 1981. 'Interviewing Women: A Contradiction in Terms'. *Doing Feminist Research*. Ed. H. Roberts. London: Routledge and Kegan Paul.

Parmar, P. 1982. 'Gender, Race and Class: Asian Women in Resistance'. *The Empire Strikes Back*. Centre for Contemporary Cultural Studies. London: Hutchinson.

Pettigrew, 1981. 'Reminiscences of Fieldwork among the Sikhs'. *Doing Feminist Research*. Ed. H. Roberts. London: Routledge and Kegan Paul.

Phizacklea, A. 1984. 'A Sociology of Migration or 'Race Relations'? A View From Britain'. *Current Sociology*. Vol. 32, no. 3, 206-218.

Phizacklea, A. 1987. 'Minority Women and Economic Restructuring'. *Work, Employment and Society*. Vol. 1, no. 3, 309-325.

Phizacklea, A. 1990. *Unpacking the Fashion Industry*. London: Routledge and Kegan Paul.

Piore, M. and C. Sabel. 1984. *The Second Industrial Divide*. New York: Basic Books.

Pollert, A. 1981. *Girls, Wives, Factory Lives*. London: Macmillan.

Pollert, A. 1991. (Ed.) *Farewell to Flexibility*. Oxford: Blackwell

Rainnie, A. 1989. *Industrial Relations in Small Firms*. London: Routledge.

Ram, M. 1988. 'Clothing in Wolverhampton'. *Local Work*. No. 8, 5-6.

Rex, J., and R. Moore. 1967. *Race, Community and Conflict*. London: Oxford University Press.

Roy, D. 1954. 'Efficiency and the "Fix": Informal Intergroup Relations in a Piecework Machine Shop'. *American Journal of Sociology*. Vol. 60, no. 3, 255-266.

Rubery, J. 1988. 'Employers and the Labour Market'. *Employment in Britain*. Ed. D. Gallie. Oxford: Blackwell.

Scase, R. and R. Goffee. 1982. "Fraternalism" and "Paternalism" as Employer Strategies in Small Firms'. *Diversity and Decomposition in the Labour Market*. Ed. G. Day with L. Caldwell, K. Jones, D. Robbins and H. Rose. Aldershot: Gower.

Scase, R., and R. Goffee. 1987. *The Real World of the Small Business Owner*. London: Routledge and Kegan Paul.

Smith, C., J. Child and M. Rowlinson. 1990. *Reshaping Work: The Cadbury Experience*. Cambridge: Cambridge University Press.

Stanworth, J., and J. Curran. 1981. 'Size of Workplace and Attitudes to Industrial Relations'. *British Journal of Industrial Relations*, Vol 1, no. 1, 14-25.

Strinati, D. 1990. 'A Ghost in the Machine ?: The State and the Labour Process in Theory and Practice'. *Labour Process Theory*. Ed. D. Knights and H. Wilmott. London: Macmillan.

Streeck, W. 1987. 'The Uncertainties of Management'. *Work, Employment and Society*. Vol. 1, no.3, 281-308.

Thompson, P. 1983. *The Nature of Work*. London: Macmillan.

Totterdill, P. and J. Zeitlin. 1989. 'Markets, Technology and Local Intervention'. *Reversing Industrial Decline: Industrial Structure and Industrial Policy in Britain and her Competitors*. Ed. P. Hirst and J. Zeitlin. Oxford: Berg.

Wallman, S. 1979. (Ed.) *Ethnicity at Work*. London: Macmillan.

Ward, R. 1987. 'Resistance, Accommodation and Advantage: Strategic Development in Ethnic Business'. *The Manufacture of Disadvantage*. Ed. G. Lee and R. Loveridge. Milton Keynes: Open University Press.

Ward, R. and Jenkins, R. 1984. (Eds.) *Ethnic Communities in Business*. London: Cambridge.

Ward, R. and R. Smith. 1987. 'Industry Context and Entrepreneurship'. Workshop on Entrepreneurship in Europe, May, 1-17.

Werbner, P. 1984. 'Business on Trust'. *Ethnic Communities in Business*. Ed. R. Ward and R. Jenkins. London: Cambridge.

West Midlands Low Pay Unit. 1991. *The Clothes Showdown: The Future of the West Midlands Clothing Industry*. Birmingham: WMPLU.

Westwood, S. 1984. *All Day Every Day*. London: Pluto.

Westwood, S. 1988. 'Workers and Wives: Continuities and Discontinuities in the Lives of Gujarati Women'. *Enterprising Women*. Ed. S. Westwood and P. Bhachu. London: Routledge and Kegan Paul.

Westwood, S. and P. Bhachu. 1988. (Eds.) Introduction. *Enterprising Women*. London: Routledge and Kegan Paul.

Wilson, A. 1976. *Finding a Voice: Asian Women in Britain*. London: Hutchinson.

Wolverhampton District Council, 1988. *The Training Needs of the Wolverhampton Clothing Industry*.

Index